CAMBRIDGE LIBRARY COLLECTION

Books of enduring scholarly value

Printing and Publishing History

The interface between authors and their readers is a fascinating subject in its own right, revealing a great deal about social attitudes, technological progress, aesthetic values, fashionable interests, political positions, economic constraints, and individual personalities. This part of the Cambridge Library Collection reissues classic studies in the area of printing and publishing history that shed light on developments in typography and book design, printing and binding, the rise and fall of publishing houses and periodicals, and the roles of authors and illustrators. It documents the ebb and flow of the book trade supplying a wide range of customers with products from almanacs to novels, bibles to erotica, and poetry to statistics.

Paper and Paper Making, Ancient and Modern

This short history of paper-making is based on lectures delivered at the London Institute, and was first published in book form in 1855. The young Richard Herring (b. 1829) covers a great deal of ground in just three chapters. His book begins with the origins of writing itself, the first materials upon which people wrote, and the mastery of Egyptian papyrus. He then describes more recent developments such as the paper-making techniques developed in the eighteenth century by James Whatman, watermarks, and an especially captivating section on how the close analysis of paper was used to expose a forgery of Shakespearean manuscripts. The introduction by the Reverend George Croly stresses the importance of paper-making and printing to Christian history. Herring writes enthusiastically, punctuating his account with anecdotes, and patriotically emphasises the unrivalled brilliance of printing in England.

T0382629

Cambridge University Press has long been a pioneer in the reissuing of out-of-print titles from its own backlist, producing digital reprints of books that are still sought after by scholars and students but could not be reprinted economically using traditional technology. The Cambridge Library Collection extends this activity to a wider range of books which are still of importance to researchers and professionals, either for the source material they contain, or as landmarks in the history of their academic discipline.

Drawing from the world-renowned collections in the Cambridge University Library, and guided by the advice of experts in each subject area, Cambridge University Press is using state-of-the-art scanning machines in its own Printing House to capture the content of each book selected for inclusion. The files are processed to give a consistently clear, crisp image, and the books finished to the high quality standard for which the Press is recognised around the world. The latest print-on-demand technology ensures that the books will remain available indefinitely, and that orders for single or multiple copies can quickly be supplied.

The Cambridge Library Collection will bring back to life books of enduring scholarly value (including out-of-copyright works originally issued by other publishers) across a wide range of disciplines in the humanities and social sciences and in science and technology.

Paper
and Paper Making,
Ancient and Modern

With an Introduction by the Rev. George Croly

RICHARD HERRING

CAMBRIDGE UNIVERSITY PRESS

Cambridge, New York, Melbourne, Madrid, Cape Town, Singapore,
São Paolo, Delhi, Dubai, Tokyo, Mexico City

Published in the United States of America by Cambridge University Press, New York

www.cambridge.org
Information on this title: www.cambridge.org/9781108009058

© in this compilation Cambridge University Press 2010

This edition first published 1855
This digitally printed version 2010

ISBN 978-1-108-00905-8 Paperback

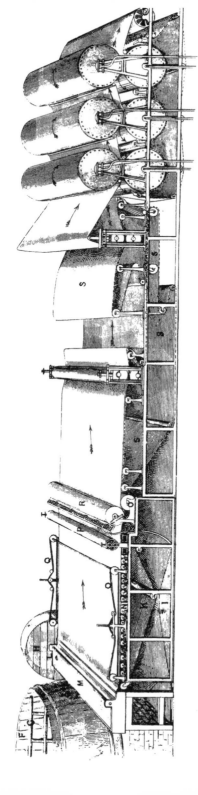

THE PAPER MAKING MACHINE

PAPER & PAPER MAKING,

ANCIENT AND MODERN.

BY

RICHARD HERRING:

WITH

AN INTRODUCTION,

BY THE

REV. GEORGE CROLY, LL. D.

LONDON:
LONGMAN, BROWN, GREEN, AND LONGMANS.

1855.

CONTENTS.

CHAPTER I.

CHAPTER II.

CHAPTER III.

PREFACE.

The present work is founded upon Lectures recently delivered at the London Institution.

The subject of Paper and Paper Making is one which has been at all times regarded with considerable interest, independently of that attention to it which commercial pursuits, of necessity, demand. The confidence, however, which originally prompted me to treat the subject, has, been in no slight degree, augmented by the advantage which I possess in the experience of my father, extending over a period of nearly half a century.

In the illustration of the Lectures, (which here stand as CHAPTERS 1 and 2),—the syllabus furnished by the London Institution being retained as a heading in each instance—I have the pleasing duty to acknowledge myself much indebted to the kind assistance of many friends in connection with the Royal Asiatic Society, the Hon. East India Company, the Royal Botanical Gardens at Kew, the London Missionary Museum, and the Bank of England.

So far as it has been found practicable to illustrate the present work, no effort has been spared, and in order to sustain the interest which was so strikingly exhibited at the delivery of the Lectures—the remembrance of which throughout life will be to me a constant source of gratification ;—I have appended, amongst other specimens, a sheet manufactured from the same mould as I then employed.

R. H.

Walbrook, April, 1855.

INTRODUCTION.

BY THE REV. GEORGE CROLY, LL. D.

HAVING been present at the delivery of these Lectures, and feeling an interest in them, as the performance of my intelligent friend, and parishioner, Mr. Herring, I have added, at his request, a few preliminary observations, on the chief employment of paper in our day, namely, in PRINTING.

It is a striking, and perhaps a significant, coincidence, that the art of making paper from linen fibre, and the art of printing, were discovered nearly at the same time, and were coeval with the first preaching of the Reformation; by Huss and Jerome of Prague, of whom Luther was only the more eminent successor—the whole three events dating from the fifteenth century.

It is certain, that printing was the great instrument of the Reformation in Germany, and of spreading it through Europe; and it is equally certain, that the making of paper, by means of the cotton or flaxen fibre, supplied the only material, which has been found extensively available for printing. Whether this coincidence was simply accidental, or was the effect of that high arrangement for high purposes, which we so often find in the history of Providence, may be left to the consideration of the Christian.

But, it is evident, that if printing had been invented in any of the earlier ages, it would have been comparatively thrown away. The Chinese bark of the bamboo, or the rice straw; the Egyptian papyrus, and the Greek or Roman parchment, would have been too feeble, or too expensive, for the rapid demands of the Press. But, at the exact period, when Printing was given to the world, the fabric was also given, which was to meet the broadest exigency of that most illustrious invention.

That the Chinese, in ages almost beyond history, had made paper of cotton, and even of hemp; and that the Arabians either borrowed, or invented, the manufacture, in the eighth century, is known. But, the discovery perished for want of the Press; as the Press would have perished for want of the vigour, yet to be created in every faculty of human advance, by the Reformation.

It should not be forgotten, that the *first* printed works were religious; as the "Biblia Pauperum," a small folio, of forty leaves, each with a picture, and a text of Scripture under it; and the "Speculum humanæ Salvationis," a similar work of pictures and texts, in Latin; and that the last, and noblest, achievement of Printing, has been the renewed publication of the Gospel, in nearly every language of the globe!

The actual origin of Printing has been matter of learned controversy. From the earliest ages, impressions had been taken from seals. There are in the British Museum blocks of lead, impressed with the name or stamp of the Roman authorities. The Chinese, who seem to have had a glimpse of every invention of Europe, produced blocks of wood-engraving, with which they multiplied copies, by impression at least, so early as the tenth century; and even appear to have applied it to a species of bank note. Whether the invention was introduced into Europe by Marco

Polo, (who visited China in the thirteenth century), or by others, it is known, that printed playing cards and devotional tracts, (though of the simplest structure, generally a single page), were not infrequent, from the year A.D. 1400. Still, the operation was so expensive, and, also, so insufficient, that the Art of Printing cannot be said, to have been yet discovered. For this discovery, the essential was the use of *moveable types*.

The honour of this most simple, yet most comprehensive, change, has been warmly disputed by Holland, and Germany. But, though Coster, a Hollander, adopted it early; general opinion gives it to Gutenburg, a printer at Strasburg, between 1436 and 1442. Gutenburg was originally a block-printer; at length the fortunate idea occurred to him, of getting rid of the solid page, and making his types separate; those, in the first instance, were cut out of wood. Returning to Mayence, his native city, a partnership with Faust supplied him with capital. Faust made a second step in the mechanical portion of the art, by casting the types in metal. A subsequent partnership with Schoeffer, Faust's son-in-law, supplied all that was wanting to the art, in his invention of the Punch for making the types. The partners subsequently quarrelled, and Gutenburg, in 1458, formed a new establishment in Mayence. The storming of the city by Adolphus of Nassau, in 1462, dispersed the workmen, and thus spread the art through Europe. It was thenceforth practised in Italy, in France, in Spain, and in England, (at Westminster, in 1475.)

The *Cologne Chronicle*, printed in 1474, states, that the first large volume produced by printing, was the Bible, (an edition of the Vulgate,) a work which cost a preparation of ten years. This edition is without date, or printer's name, but is supposed to have been completed in 1455.

In an age, when the European mind was only emerging from a thousand years of darkness, everything was tinged with superstition. The *printing* of the Bible shared the general charge; and the comparative cheapness, and still more, the singular fidelity of the copies to each other, were attributed to sorcery. Faust, who probably had no objection to a report, by which so much was to be gained, and which was favoured by the absence of date and name; has since been made the hero of German mysticism; and is immortalized, as the philosopher, and master of magic, in the celebrated poem of Goethe.

The Newspaper, the most influential of all human works, is the *creation* of Printing. It is to the honour of England, that in this country, it approaches nearest to excellence, in intellectual vigour, in variety of knowledge, in extent of information, and in patriotic principle. It has, like all the works of man, occasional imperfections, and perhaps among the most prominent, are its too minute details of offences against public purity. But, there is scarcely a newspaper in this age, which would not have been regarded as a triumph of ability, in the last. In fact, the newspaper of England is the great practical teacher of the people. Its constant and universal teaching alone accounts for the superior intelligence of the population. Schools, lecture-rooms, and universities, important as they all are, altogether fall behind it in public effect, or find, that to retain their influence, they must follow its steps. Those steps may now and then turn from the right road, but their native tendency is, forwards and upwards! This intellectual giant always advances, and carries the country with him to a height, which no other country, ancient or modern, ever attained, or perhaps, ever hoped to attain.

I speak of this form of publication, in no literary favoritism; but, as a great instrument, offered to nations for the safety, the speed, and the security of national progress; an intellectual railroad, given to our era, to meet the increased exigencies of intellectual intercourse; and equal to any weight, and any rapidity.

The most hopeless feature of foreign governments appears to me, their hostility to the *press*. Thus, they prohibit the mental air and exercise, which would rectify the "peccant humours" of their people; thus, they aggravate popular stagnation into political disease; thus, casual passion is darkened into conspiracy, and passing disgust is compressed into rebellion.

England has her ill-humours, but the press ventilates them away; the vapours are not suffered to lie on the ground, until they condense into malaria. There may be folly, and even faction, among us, and the press may be the trumpet of both; but, the width of the area is the remedy. A *whole* nation is always right. No sound can stir it, but the sound which is in accord with its own feelings; the trumpet which is overwhelming within four walls, is unheard at the horizon!

If, in an age of foreign convulsion, England has undergone no catastrophe; if, in the fall of monarchies, she has preserved her hereditary throne; if, in the mingled infidelity and superstition of the Continent, which, like the mingled frenzy and fetters of a lunatic hospital, have, in our day, exhibited the lowest humiliation of human nature; she has preserved her freedom and her religion; I attribute all, under God, to the vigour, and intelligence of public investigation; the incessant urgency of appeal to the public mind; the living organization, of which the heart is the PRESS of England!

PAPER AND PAPER MAKING,

ANCIENT AND MODERN.

CHAPTER I.

Introduction.—Language.— Origin of the Art of Writing.—Various modes of recording events which preceded it.—Materials upon which Men first Wrote—Stones, Bricks, Metals, Skins and Intestines of Animals, Tablets, Leaves, Bark, etc., etc.—The Egyptian Papyrus, from which Paper (so called) was first made.— Process of Manufacture.— Usual dimensions and extreme durability of Papyri.—Modern Paper.— Its general advantages to mankind.—Supposed period of its Invention.— The Introduction of Paper-making into Europe.—Historical incidents connected therewith.—James Whatman.—The superiority of his manufacture.—Adoption of the Fourdrinier-Machine.—General advantages of Machinery over the Original Process, etc., etc.

Amongst the numerous and diversified objects of human investigation and research, it would, perhaps, be difficult to single out one, more curious and interesting, than that of the medium which bears the symbols of language ; which retains the register of circumstances and events of past ages, and which hands down to us the transactions of primeval time, with its intervening periods.

Undoubtedly the noblest acquisition of mankind, perhaps the greatest advantage which we possess, is that of the faculty of speech. Without speech, man, in the midst of crowds, would be

B

solitary. The endearments of friendship, and the communications of wisdom, alike would become unavailing; man, in fact, without speech, could hardly be accounted a rational being.

That the use of speech or language was given to Adam immediately upon his formation, we have no reason to doubt; for from the testimony of Moses it appears, that he not only gave names to every living creature, "to every beast of the field, and to every fowl of the air," as they were brought to him, but that also as soon as Eve was made he could say—"This is now bone of my bone, and flesh of my flesh," the first sentence which is recorded of his uttering, and which is sufficient to show, that even then, he possessed a competent stock of words to declare the ideas or conceptions of his mind.

Thus was man at once rendered as superior to the brute creation, as in after times by the aid of writing, or the art of drawing those ideas into vision, he was especially distinguished from the condition of uncivilized savages. For of all the arts that contribute to the comfort and happiness of mankind, no one, perhaps, is more intimately connected with our social habits, or more closely entwined with the best and purest feelings of our nature, than that of writing. And yet to conceive or to account for the origin

of an art so invaluable in its tendency to elevate
and improve mankind, as that of exhibiting to
sight the various conceptions of the mind, which
have no corporeal forms, by means of hiero-
glyphics or legible characters, is still as difficult
and perplexing, as in past ages it has ever proved
to the sagacity of mankind. With the poet of
old we have yet to enquire—

> " Whence did the wondrous mystic art arise,
> Of painting speech, and speaking to the eyes ?
> That we by tracing magic lines are taught
> How to embody, and to colour thought."

Notwithstanding the great and manifold bles-
sings which men have received from this
curious and wonderful invention, it is very
remarkable, as a distinguished writer observes,
that writing, which gives a sort of immor-
tality to all other things, should, by the dis-
posal of Divine Providence, be without any trace
of the memory of its first founders. Indeed, the
invention of letters and their various combina-
tions in forming words, amounting, it is computed,
to 620,448,401,733,239,439,360,000, without repeating any combination capable of being made
from so small a number of letters as that now com-
prising our alphabet, has something so extremely
ingenious and surprising in its application, that
most men who have treated the subject, can
hardly forbear attributing it to a divine original.

Many have conceived that the theatre of this important legacy to man was Mount Sinai. But it is observable, that previously to the arrival of the Israelites at Mount Sinai, Scripture makes mention of writing as an art already understood by Moses : "And the Lord said unto Moses, *write* this for a memorial." (Exodus, 17th ch. 14th v.) Now, Moses seems to have expressed no difficulty of comprehension when he received this command, nor does anything appear to induce the slightest doubt; on the contrary, I think we may safely conclude that Moses was even then well acquainted with the art of writing, or otherwise he would have been instructed by God, as in the case of Noah, when he was required to build the Ark. And further, we find that Moses wrote all the words, and all the judgments of the Lord, contained in the twenty-first and two following chapters of the Book of Exodus, before the two written tables of stone were even so much as promised. The delivery of the tables is not mentioned till the 18th verse of the 31st chapter, after God had made an end of communing with him upon the mount. Nevertheless, I am not prepared to dispute the probability of a divine origin to so wonderful a medium, any more than I am disposed to question the possibility of its resulting merely from what Aristotle terms the

Faculty of Imitation; for which, says he, men are so remarkable, even in an uncivilized state. I pass by all questions of the kind, satisfied for the present with the simple fact, that such medium does exist; that through it we become, as it were, introduced to the multitudinous throng of a world's tenantry, while we thus learn their words, works, and ways, their History, Literature, and Arts, their Science, and Theology; and while even the mummy, recovered from the subterranean recesses of the Egyptian pyramids, may still be said to talk with us, by virtue of the roll of papyrus and its pictured inscription which he holds in his hand;

> Writing's art, which like a sovereign queen,
> Amongst her subject sciences is seen ;
> As she in dignity the rest transcends,
> So far her power of good, and harm extends.

In the earliest ages of mankind, very simple means were necessarily adopted, to preserve the remembrance of any important event. During many centuries, tradition, perhaps solely, served to represent that, which in recent times has been more completely effected by the introduction of printing.

At other periods we find trees were planted, heaps of stones, altars or pillars, as we read in sacred history, were erected; and even games and festivals ordered, to keep up the recollection of important facts. Since, however, the art of writing was invented (be the period when it may), various materials have from time to time been made use of, for the purpose of transmitting to posterity the discoveries and deeds of their ancestors. Thus, for instance, the most ancient remains of writing which have been handed down to us, are upon hard substances, such as bricks, stones, and metals, which were used by the ancients for all matters of public notoriety; abundant proofs of which we have in the recent discoveries of Mr. Layard. And Josephus, in the third chapter of the first book of Jewish Antiquities, tells us: that, "the descendants of Seth, leading a happy and quiet life, found out by study and observation the motions and distribution, or order, of the heavenly bodies; and, that their discoveries might not be lost to men (knowing that the destruction of the world had been foretold by Adam, which should be once by fire, and once by water,) they made two pillars—one of brick, and the other of stone, and wrote or engraved their discoveries thereon; so that if the rains should destroy that of brick, the other of stone might continue to show mankind their observations."

In the sacred text we are further informed, that great stones were directed to be set up by the children of Israel, after the passage of the Jordan, and being "plastered with plaster,"—

which appears to have been a very common
practice—"thereon were to be written all the
words of the law very plainly." In the book
of Job, which some suppose to have been
written by Moses, we have an obscure intima-
tion of the method employed in registering upon
the rock, "graven with an iron pen and lead
in the rock for ever." But, although there is
apparently a want of clearness in our translation
of the passage, by no means does it affect the idea
of Job's desire to give the greatest possible per-
manence to the words he then uttered. He
exclaims, "Oh that my words were now written,"
or, (though probably not an exact translation,)
"Oh that they were printed in a book;" and
more (he adds) "that they were even graven with
an iron pen and lead in the rock for ever;" which
latter clause some take to be in reference to the
leaden tablets which are found to have been in
very early use. But I rather favour the inter-
pretation, for which I am indebted, to my much
esteemed friend the Rev. Dr. Croly; that as a
still more indelible and effectual mode of per-
petuating his thoughts, it was Job's conception
that his words should be graven in the rock with
an iron pen, or tool, and the interstices afterwards filled with lead, in order that the contrast
occasioned thereby might render them the more

readily intelligible to those who happened to travel that way.

Herodotus also mentions a letter engraven on plates of stone, which Themistocles, the Athenian general, sent to the Ionians, about five hundred years before the birth of Christ. Lead, however, and similar metals being less difficult to write upon, and more simple and convenient, afterwards superseded to a great extent the use of such unwieldy substances as bricks and stone. And subsequently we find others of a still more pliable texture employed, such as the skins of animals, bark, wood, and the leaves of trees. Solomon, for instance, in the Book of Proverbs, in allusion to the practice of writing upon thin slices of wood, advises his son to write his precepts upon the *tables* of his heart. And the prophet Habakkuk was commanded to write a vision and make it plain upon *tables*, that he may run that readeth it. Solomon, as you are aware, lived a thousand years, and Habakkuk about six hundred and twenty six, before the Christian era. At a later period, Zacharias, the father of John the Baptist, when enquired of as to what he would have his child called, asked, we are told, for "a *writing table*, and wrote, saying, his name is John." Amongst the Romans, it was customary for the public affairs of every year to be committed to writing by the high priest, and published on a table; such tables being exposed to view, either in their market-places or temples, in order that the people might have an opportunity of becoming acquainted with their contents.

At an early period in their history, both Greeks and Romans appear to have commonly used either those plain wooden boards, or boards covered with wax. It is probable, that at first the tables were written upon just as they were planed, and that the overlaying them with wax was an improvement on that invention. A very decided advantage being thus obtained, in the facility afforded for erasing any inaccuracies that might have occurred, and consequently of correcting the manuscript. The practice of writing upon tablets of one kind or another, appears not to have been entirely laid aside, until the commencement of the fourteenth century; and, indeed, even in our day, tablet books of ivory are occasionally used, for writing upon with black lead pencils.

The use of *boards* was in some measure superseded by that of the leaves of palm, olive, poplar, and other trees. And, although in Europe, all these disappeared upon the introduction of the papyrus and parchments, in some countries the use of them remains even to this day. Perhaps a record of this old custom may still be found in the word *leaf*, which we continue to apply to sheets of paper, when sewed up into the form of a book. According to the account of Pliny, the Egyptians were the first to use the palm leaf, and books written on it are still preserved in the East India Museum, as also in the Library of the British Museum.

The mode of preparation, after cutting into strips of the length and width required, is simply to soak them for a short time in boiling water, after which they are rubbed backwards and forwards over a smooth piece of wood to make them pliable, and then carefully dried. The letters or characters being written or rather engraved thereon with an iron style, which, piercing the outside covering, makes indelible letters; and by afterwards rubbing the writing over with some dark coloured substance, such as soot or charcoal, the parts etched or scratched, have greater relief imparted to them : and the writing is more easily read.

Notwithstanding many paper mills have been erected in India, the natives, I understand, frequently prefer this method, not only for the ordinary purposes of correspondence and accounts, but even in some quarters for government documents of importance.

I must here express my sense of the kind assistance which has on several occasions been afforded me by the Rev. Benjamin Bailey, late of Cottyam, Allepie, Madras, who has not only given to the world a translation in Malayalim of the entire Bible, but has also compiled two voluminous dictionaries, for rendering assistance in the study of that language. This gentleman has recently afforded me an opportunity of inspecting many great curiosities of the kind: indeed, before me is now lying a very neat little specimen written in Malayalim by him (St. Paul's Second Epistle to Timothy), which shows, in a remarkable degree, the astonishing distinctness which may be produced by this singular mode of writing.

The style with which the letters are engraven upon the leaf is usually worn in the girdle as a prominent ornament of dress. The case which protects it containing also a small knife, employed in preparing the slips, and likewise a little instrument which is used for piercing the leaves, in order that cords may be passed through them for the purpose of securing the manuscript, as may be seen in the instance of various documents both in the East India Company's Museum, and also in the Library of the British Museum.

A work which I possess, termed the *Kamma-*

vakyam, written in the Pali language, in Burmese character, upon palm leaf, is thus secured between very handsome covers. It is a Catechism of Sacred Rites, used by the Buddhist priesthood in the examination of a candidate for admission to that order. A translation of it here, however, would be no more consistent in point of matter contained, than it would be in reference to the subject I am treating. Its character and language throughout are truly humiliating to human nature.

In the British Museum there are many very singular documents of the kind, one in particular, which is written upon 390 leaves, bound, as it were, in a frame of gilt copper in the form of a tortoise, screws being passed through the strips instead of cords, the fastenings, with some addition, representing the limbs of the animal. And in the East India Museum may be seen a smaller one, protected by stout wooden covers, which has been carved to represent some animal, apparently a pig. The custom of writing upon leaves of trees, appears to have given rise to the adoption also of the interior bark; the outer being seldom made use of, in consequence of its extreme coarseness. When employed, it is customarily folded over, to admit of its being written upon both sides. The only documents of this kind,

which have come under my notice, have been
Batta manuscripts, from the island of Sumatra.

Before the art of making paper was known to
the Chinese, they appear to have cut pieces of
silk to such sizes as they wished to make their
books, and thereupon painted the letters with
pencils; the silk being first steeped in a kind of
size, to prevent the colour from running. But
such material being liable to decay, various
animal substances were afterwards employed,
as being of a more durable nature. Of course
the skins were principally used, after being
tanned; but their bones, and even entrails, were
also made use of for the like purpose. Thus, in
the " History of Mahomet," we read that the
Arabians used the shoulder bones of sheep, on
which they carved remarkable events with a knife,
when, after tying them with a string, they hung
those chronicles up in their cabinets. And in the
library of Ptolemy Philadelphus, which is said to
have contained 700,000 volumes, were the works
of Homer, written in golden letters, on the skins
of serpents. I might mention, that the term
volume here, should not be understood in the sense
which it is now customary to receive it, but
in its derivation from the Latin; signifying
simply a roll, which was the most ancient form of
book.

Parchment, or the skins of beasts, dressed and prepared in a manner rendering them fit for writing upon, appears to have been employed at a very early period. Diodorus Siculus informs us, that the Persians of old wrote all their records on skins; and Herodotus also alludes to sheep skins, and goat skins, as in general use among the Ionians about 440 years before the Christian Era. The word Parchment is a corruption of the Latin *Pergamena*, from *Pergamus*, which some allege to have been the place of its invention. But it is very probable that in the time of Eumenes, who was king of Pergamus, (about 200 years before Christ,) the circumstance of increased consumption merely occasioned the discovery of a better method of dressing the skins; from which fact alone, and perhaps with sufficient reason, the origin of the present term was derived. Eumenes, about that period, appears to have endeavoured to form a library at Pergamus, which should surpass that of Ptolemy Philadelphus at Alexandria, and in so doing enraged Ptolemy to that degree, that he immediately prohibited any further exportation from Egypt, of the papyrus which by that time was coming into very general use, and thus effectually put a stop to Eumenes' emulation in that particular. It may be, however, that this prohibition was not solely occasioned by jealousy, but by Ptolemy's fearing that his dominions, which were so much improved in arts, sciences, and civilization, since the discovery and adoption of the papyrus, (of which we shall presently speak), would be again reduced to a state of ignorance for want of it; the plant sometimes failing in unfavourable weather, while the supply invariably proved unequal to the demand. The people of Pergamus, therefore, were obliged to devise other means, and the improved manufacture of parchment would seem to have been the result. But, that Eumenes on this occasion invented the art of making parchment is exceedingly dubious; for in the books of Isaiah, Jeremiah, Ezekiel, and other parts of Scripture, we find mention made of rolls of writing: in all probability rolls of parchment.

The manner of reading such rolls may be gathered from a passage extracted from Hartley's "Travels in Greece," which serves also to elucidate the peculiar scriptural expression of their being "written within and without." You began, (says he) to read by unfolding, and you continued to read and to unfold, till, at last, you arrived at the stick to which the roll was attached; then you turned the parchment round, and continued to read on the other side of the roll, folding it gradually up until you completed the writing, thus were they " written within and without."

Papyrus, from which the term paper was derived, is the name of a celebrated plant, once extensively used by the Egyptians for making various articles of utility, such as baskets, shoes, cordage, and the like. Some writers state that of this plant the little ark was made, in which the parents of Moses exposed him upon the banks of the Nile, and of this it was that the most ancient paper was manufactured. Not as would now be customary, by first reducing it to a pulp, nor, indeed, in any way as resembling modern paper, except that in both, vegetable fibre is the basis. That a plant once so useful, and for ages in Egypt so commercially valuable, should have totally disappeared, being altogether unknown to modern botanists, appears scarcely credible; yet so it is. For the ancient descriptions of the papyrus, as a flag or bulrush, with a triangular stem that could barely be spanned, and which grew to the height of ten feet, or even considerably more, in the immense marshes occupying a large part of the surface of lower Egypt; a leafless wood, as it were, or as one writer describes it, a forest without branches, the bare stem being surmounted only by a head of long, thin, straight fibres, is certainly quite irreconcilable with the nature of the plant which now bears that name, and of which one of the stoutest growth has been very kindly furnished me by Sir W. J. Hooker, from the Royal Gardens at Kew.

In the prophecy of Isaiah a very remarkable prediction occurs with reference to this plant. " The paper reeds by the brooks, by the mouth of the brooks, and everything sown by the brooks, shall wither, be driven away, and be no more." Doubtless, we may believe that this prophecy has literally received its fulfilment.

With reference to the mode in which the paper was manufactured from this plant, two distinct opinions have been handed down to us. One, that the epidermis being removed, the spongy part was cut into thin slices, which were steeped in the waters of the Nile, or in water slightly imbued with gum; after which two layers were placed one above another, carefully arranged in contrary directions, that is, lengthwise and breadthwise, which, after being dried, were finally smoothed and brought to a fit surface for receiving writing, by being rubbed with a tooth or piece of polished ivory.

Another method said to have been adopted in preparing this material, was simply that of separating the thin concentric coats, or pellicles of the plant which surrounded the

c

stock, by means of a needle or pointed shell (on an average about twenty from each stalk), and afterwards extending them longitudinally side by side on a table, a similar layer being placed across them at right angles; in which state they were moistened with water, and while wet put under pressure, being afterwards exposed to the rays of the sun, and finally polished as in the former case, with some hard substance, such as a tooth or shell, not merely for the purpose of improving the surface, but to prevent its absorbing the ink. The saccharine matter with which the whole juice of the plant is said to have been impregnated, being usually sufficient to cause the adhesion of the strips together.

So great was the importance of this manufacture at some periods, that Gibbon informs us of one Firmus, who raised the standard of revolt in Egypt against the Emperor Aurelian; that he boasted he would maintain an army solely from the profits of his paper trade. At another time, in the reign of Tiberius, there happened such a scarcity of paper, from causes that are not mentioned, that the Senate, in order to prevent a riot, were obliged to appoint commissioners to distribute paper to the applicants according to their respective demands.

Papyri vary much more in length than in

breadth, and upon this fact I would dwell, as decidedly favouring the conception that the outer coat merely was employed in preparing the writing material. Indeed, in every specimen which I have examined, I have found the slips of which it is composed rarely exceeding twelve or fifteen inches even lengthwise. Whereas, if they had been produced from the pithy part of the stem, after being cut into slices, there would have been no difficulty whatever in manufacturing the paper of the entire length, which, as I have already stated, sometimes exceeded ten feet.

The breadth of papyri seldom exceeds eighteen inches, sometimes they are not more than four inches in width, which I imagine to have been determined by the length of the outer coats or pellicles taken from the plant; the length, of course, being carried to any extent, simply by fastening one sheet to another. The largest specimen of which I have heard is one at Paris, measuring thirty feet in length. The most interesting which we possess in this country is one which may be seen in the Manuscript Department of the British Museum, which appears to have been written in Latin in the year 572, upon a roll of papyrus, eight feet and a half long, and twelve inches wide. It is a deed relating to the sale of a house and land at Ravenna.

Though papyri found on mummies are often in a good state of preservation, it is necessary to be very careful in handling them. The roll, owing to its being pressed under the swathings of the mummy, being completely flattened, and from the unvarying high temperature of the tomb to which it has for so long a time been subjected, is frequently so dry and brittle, that if any attempt be made to unroll it without previous precaution, small pieces will continually fall off. Still, the durability of this writing material is one of its best qualities. It can, in some instances, be rolled and unrolled after the lapse of many centuries without any detriment to it; but the complete preservation of such specimens is generally to be attributed to their being kept from the air either in wooden or earthen vessels, frequently in the interior of the Idol to which the mummy was once wont to present his offering, which is usually of some grotesque, or even hideous form, altogether unworthy of mention as representing any created thing, either upon the face of the earth, or in the waters beneath. Not long since I was shown one, containing a roll of papyrus, which had been roughly carved out of wood, somewhat resembling an overgrown *cat* in a sitting posture. And this so called god, as appears to have been customarily the case, was taken from the tomb, where it stood over the mummy, with two very beautiful vases, which at one time contained fragrant oils, believed to be acceptable to the Idol, placed in front. The papyri thus curiously preserved, usually contain an account of the rank or station which the dead once filled, and occasionally some description of the particular rites and ceremonies observed with reference to the worship.

With respect to the period at which the ancients began to make a writing substance of the papyrus, or, indeed, of the name of the originator, nothing decisive is known. It would, however, appear from the prophecy in Isaiah, which has been already referred to, in which mention is made of paper reeds by the brooks, that paper made of such reeds was actually in use when that prophecy was written. And in accordance with this conception, the learned Dr. Gill, in his commentary says, "On the banks of the Nile grew a reed, or rush, called by the Greeks papyrus, or byblus, from whence come the words paper and bible, or book, of which paper was anciently made, even as early as the time of Isaiah," now nearly 3000 years ago.

The kind of pen ordinarily used for writing upon this material was simply *a reed*, cut and split just as our quill pens at present are, but with a point not quite so sharp.

I have in my possession some very fine specimens of what is usually called Bark Cloth, which, in its manufacture, approximates more nearly to that of modern paper than any other substance with which I am acquainted. It is formed from the bark of a small tree, or shrub, called the Paper Mulberry *(morus papyrifera)*, which grows wild in the southern provinces of China, in Ava, in the Burmese country, and in India, as well as in all the Asiatic and Polynesian· islands from Japan to Otaheite. If a strip of this bark, which is remarkable for the fineness of its texture, after being soaked in water, be laid on a smooth stone, and then carefully beaten with a bat or mallet, the surface of which is cut into fine ribs, the fibres will become separated more or less from one another, and if the beating be carefully conducted, the bark will ultimately assume the appearance of a web of fine linen, two pieces of bark being made to incorporate with one another simply by laying them so as to overlap a little, and then beating again. In this simple way the material is formed; and by a short exposure to the sunshine when wet, becomes perfectly white. To. render it fit for writing, it is afterwards polished in a manner similar to the papyrus, by rubbing it with a shell or other hard substance until it has very much the appearance of parchment; and that it bears ink perfectly well, may be seen by an inspection of some Javanese Works, which are contained in the library of the Hon. East India Company.

The bat or mallet employed by the natives in preparing this material is usually about 15 inches in length, and from two and a half to three inches square, one side being grooved very coarsely, another somewhat finer, a third exceedingly fine, and the fourth generally cut in chequers or small squares. The bark is first beaten with the coarsest side of the instrument, and then, in turn, with those parts which are finer, the resinous matter contained in it being usually found sufficiently adhesive.

Without, however, dwelling longer upon this portion of our subject, which time will not permit, let us now proceed to trace out, in some measure, the history and progress of that more perfect and ingenious invention, MODERN PAPER; and in so doing, I can hardly forbear making some allusion to the incalculable advantages which have resulted to mankind from the introduction of so ingenious and extraordinary a discovery. It certainly would appear very re-

markable, that not only amongst mankind generally, but even with those intimately associated
with that branch of commerce, so little interest
should be found to exist in an acquaintance with
its origin and advancement, beyond the bare
knowledge which directly concerns them. It is
true that with them, no less than with people in
general, the very indispensableness of the material
renders familiarity at once an unconscious stum-
bling-block, to any conception of the grandeur
of its importance, or its vastly interesting, and
varied associations. Yet what infinite trouble
and labour, what fruitless consumption of time, has
not been saved by the invention of paper. How
many toilsome and dangerous experiments have
not philosophical projectors been spared. What
laborious investigations and study have not thus
been abridged, by the facts of others' researches
being so conveyed to posterity—knowledge,
more than any one man could have attained to
in a thousand years, though born with faculties
in maturity. To enumerate all the advantages
which the invention of paper has afforded mankind, it were, indeed, useless to attempt; for,
whether we look at the traveller, traversing sea
and land, without the knowledge of geography,
and navigation; without those beautiful charts of
the ocean, by which he is now enabled to proceed

with safety, and even to predict with certainty, his
arrival at the most distant ports : or, whether we
look at the man of science, who being neither
artist, nor manufacturer, is thus enabled to com-
municate his plans and projects with accuracy
and ease, for mechanics afterwards to improve
and perfect: or, indeed, whether we view the
growing youth, educated with such facility in the
principles of their duty, backward even to bar-
barous states, softened and enlightened by means
of the discovery; its value, in the applicability
of its purposes, stands out alike in each, declaring
it distinctly above all other inventions, as truly
the most wonderful, useful, and important, which
has ever yet transpired in any age of the world ;
inasmuch, as without it, every other discovery
must necessarily have continued comparatively
useless to society.   For, be it remembered, that
in contrasting the results of this invention, with
the productions of former periods, we are, in fact,
arraying in our train, the mighty arm of the
press against the feeble efforts of an unwieldy
style, or the tedious and uncertain process of the
slow-paced pen, which prior to an acquaintance
with the art of printing, were the only means
mankind possessed for spreading the influence
and advantages of learning amongst their fellow-

creatures. And, again, how highly interesting is it, to observe the prodigious advancement resulting from an ingenious and successful application of machinery in the one case, serving at the same time to develop to our wonder and amazement the extraordinary capabilities of production which have since been revealed by the Printing Machine. Truly may we now pronounce—

> The Press! the venerated Press!
> Freedom's impenetrable shield—
> The sword that wins her best success,
> The only sword that man should wield.

It is stated that the daily aggregate printed surface of the *Times* alone, actually exceeds that of thirty acres, and the *Illustrated London News,* on one occasion, sent forth no less than 500,000 double numbers, or one million sheets. In fact, 2000 reams, exceeding seventy tons in weight.

The manufacture of four or five hundred square feet of paper per minute, and 12,000 impressions per hour, are now matters of every day occurrence, although it should be borne in mind, that without the *paper machine*, pouring forth its miles of web, these corresponding advantages in printing could not have been developed.

We may take as an instance, that book of books, which Pollok very beautifully describes as—

> " The only star
> By which the bark of man could navigate
> The sea of life, and gain the coast of bliss
> Securely !''

Although now a handsome copy, printed on tolerably fine paper, gilt edged, and bound in embossed roan, may be purchased for one shilling, in the reign of Henry the Third, it is recorded that two arches of London Bridge were built for a less sum than that for which a Bible could be procured. And, as we continue the search still further back, the contrast becomes increasingly interesting. For let it be remembered, that the sixty-six books of which the Bible is composed, were not always contained in so convenient a form. During the sixteen centuries which were occupied in making known this revelation to man, not only were the advantages which we possess altogether unknown, even in their rudest form, but substitutes, apparently far less promising than many we have referred to, were also at one period and another directed to be employed. As for instance, to Ezekiel, Jehovah once said, " Thou also son of man, take thee a *tile*, and lay it before thee, and pourtray upon it the city, even Jerusalem." And elsewhere, " More-

over, thou son of man, take thee one *stick*, and
write upon it, for Judah, and for the children of
Israel, his companions.

Of course there have been occasions when certain portions of the Scriptures were very beautifully inscribed (more particularly of the New
Testament) sometimes in letters of gold, on parchment of the richest purple. Still they were *manuscript*, and as such, not unfrequently occupied the
labour of individuals for years. Instances are
upon record, of fifty years in the life of one man
being engaged in the execution of a single copy of
the Scriptures. In the present day it is, perhaps,
impossible for us properly to appreciate the skill,
the labour, and the immense expenditure employed in such productions.

For now, by the aid of the printing machine, we
have an entire copy struck off in the space of one
minute ; and such were the almost miraculous
efforts of the British and Foreign Bible Society
last year, that they actually issued, in nearly 150
known languages, an average circulation of a copy
for every minute throughout the year.

It is much to be regretted that in tracing
the origin of so curious an art as that of the manufacture of modern paper, any definite conclusion as to the precise time or period of its adoption should hitherto have proved altogether

unattainable. The Royal Society of Sciences at Gottingen, in 1755 and 1763, offered considerable premiums for that especial object, but unfortunately all researches, however directed, were utterly fruitless. The most ancient manuscript on *cotton paper* appears to have been written in 1050, while Eustathius, who wrote towards the end of the 12th century, states that the Egyptian papyrus had gone into disuse but a little before his time. To reconcile, however, in some measure contradictory accounts, it may be observed, that on some particular occasions, and by some particular persons, the Egyptian paper might have been employed for several hundred years after it ceased to be in general use, and it is quite certain, that although the new invention must have proved of great advantage to mankind, it could only have been introduced by degrees. Amongst the records which are preserved at the Tower of London I have seen a letter addressed to Henry the Third, and written previously to 1222, which appears to be upon strong paper, of mixed materials. Several letters of the following reign, which are there preserved, are evidently written on *cotton* paper. Were we able to determine the precise time when paper was first made from cotton, we should also be enabled to fix the invention of the art of paper making

as it is now practised. For the application of
cotton to the purposes of paper making, requires
almost as much labour and ingenuity as the use
of linen rags. Some have conceived, and I think
with sufficient reason, that China originally gave
birth to the invention. Certain it is, that the art
of making paper from vegetable matter reduced
to pulp was known and understood there long
before it was practised in Europe, which did not
take place until the 11th century, and the Chinese have carried it to a high degree of perfection. Several kinds of their paper evince the
greatest art and ingenuity, and are applied with
much advantage to many purposes. One especially, manufactured from the inner bark of the
bamboo, is particularly celebrated for affording
the clearest and most delicate impressions from
copper plates, which we ordinarily term *india
proofs*. The Chinese, however, make paper of
various kinds, some of the bark of trees, especially the mulberry tree, and the elm, but chiefly
of the bamboo and cotton tree, and occasionally
from other substances, such as hemp, wheat, or
rice straw. To give an idea of the manner of
fabricating paper from these different substances,
it will suffice, (the process being nearly the same
in each,) to confine our observations to the method adopted in the manufacture of paper from

the bamboo,—a kind of cane or hollow reed, divided by knots, but larger, more elastic, and more durable than any other reed. The whole substance of the bamboo is at times employed by the Chinese in this operation, but the younger stalks are preferred. The canes being first cut into pieces of four or five feet in length, are made into parcels, and thrown into a reservoir of mud and water for about a fortnight, to soften them; they are then taken out, and carefully washed, every one of the pieces being again cut into filaments, which are exposed to the rays of the sun to dry, and to bleach. After this they are boiled in large kettles, and then reduced to pulp in mortars, by means of a hammer with a long handle; or as is more commonly the case, by submitting the mass to the action of stampers, raised in the usual way by cogs on a revolving axis. The pulp being thus far prepared, a glutinous substance, extracted from the shoots of a certain plant, is next mixed with it in stated quantities, and upon this mixture chiefly depends the quality of the paper. As soon as this has taken place the whole is again beaten together until it becomes a thick viscous liquor, which, after being reduced to an essential state of consistency, by a further admixture of water, is then transferred to a large reservoir or vat, having on each side of it a drying stove, in the form of the ridge of a house, that is, consisting of two sloping sides touching at top. These sides are covered externally with an exceedingly smooth coating of stucco, and a flue passes through the brickwork, so as to keep the whole of each side equally and moderately warm. A vat and a stove are placed alternately in the manufactory, so that there are two sides of two different stoves adjacent to each vat. The workman dips his mould, which is sometimes formed merely of bulrushes, cut in narrow strips, and mounted in a frame, into the vat, and then raises it out again, the water passing off through the perforations in the bottom, and the pulpy paperstuff remaining on its surface. The frame of the mould is then removed, and the bottom is pressed against the side of one of the stoves, so as to make the sheet of paper adhere to its surface, and allow the sieve, (as it were) to be withdrawn. The moisture, of course, speedily evaporates by the warmth of the stove, but before the paper is quite dry, it is brushed over on its outer surface with a size made of rice, which also soon dries, and the paper is then stripped off in a finished state, having one surface exquisitely smooth, it being seldom the practice of the Chinese to write or print on both sides of the paper.

While all this is taking place, the moulder has made a second sheet, and pressed it against the side of the other stove, where it undergoes the operation of sizing and drying, precisely as in the former case.

The very delicate material, which is brought from China in pieces only a few inches square, and commonly, but erroneously, termed *rice paper*, is in reality but a membrane of the bread-fruit tree, obtained by cutting the stem spirally round the axis, and afterwards flattening it by pressure. That it is not an artificial production may very readily be perceived by contrasting one of the more translucent specimens with a piece of the finest manufactured paper, by the aid of the microscope.

The precise period at which the manufacture of paper was first introduced into Europe appears to be rather a matter of uncertainty. Paper-mills, moved by water power, were in operation in Tuscany at the commencement of the fourteenth century; and at Nuremberg, in Germany, one was established in 1390, by Ulman Stromer, who wrote the first work ever published on the art of paper making. He seems to have employed a great number of persons, all of whom were obliged to take an oath that they would not teach any one the art of paper making, or make it on their own account. In the following year, when anxious to increase the means of its production, he met with such strong opposition from those he employed, who would not consent to any enlargement of the mill, that it became at length requisite to bring them before the magistrates, by whom they were imprisoned, after which they submitted, by renewing their oaths. Two or three centuries later, we find the Dutch in like manner, so extremely jealous with respect to the manufacture, as to prohibit the exportation of moulds, under no less severe a penalty than that of death.

Fuller makes some exceedingly curious observations respecting the paper of his time, which may, perhaps, be introduced here with advantage. He says—"Paper participates in some sort of the character of the country which makes it; the Venetian being neat, subtile, and court like; the French light, slight, and slender; and the Dutch thick, corpulent, and gross, sucking up the ink with the sponginess thereof." He complains that the paper manufactories were not then sufficiently encouraged, considering the vast sums of money expended in our land for paper out of Italy, France, and Germany, which might be lessened, were it made in our nation. "To such who object," says he, "that we can never equal the perfection of Venice paper, I return, neither can we match the purity of Venice glasses, and yet many green ones are blown in Sussex, profitable to the makers, and convenient to the users, our home-spun paper might be found beneficial."

With reference to any particular *time* or *place* at which this inestimable invention was first adopted in England, all researches into existing records contribute little to our assistance. The first paper mill erected here is commonly attributed to Sir John Spielman, a German, who established one in 1588, at Dartford, for which the honour of knighthood was afterwards conferred upon him by Queen Elizabeth, who was also pleased to grant him a license "for the sole gathering for ten years of all rags, &c., necessary for the making of such paper." It is, however, quite certain that paper mills were in existence here long before Spielman's time. Shakespeare, in the second part of his play of Henry the Sixth, the plot of which appears laid at least a century previously, refers to a paper mill. In fact, he introduces it as an additional weight to the charge which Jack Cade is made to bring against Lord Say, "Thou hast most traitorously corrupted," says he, "the youth of the realm, in erecting a grammar school, and whereas, before, our forefathers had no other books but the score and the tally, thou hast caused printing to be used, and contrary to the king, his crown and dignity, thou hast built a paper mill."

Understanding that some five-and-thirty or forty years since it was asserted by the then occupier of North Newton mill, near Banbury, in Oxfordshire, which at that time was the property of Lord Saye and Sele, that such was the first erected in this country for the manufacture of paper, and also that it was to that mill Shakspeare referred in the passage just quoted, I recently communicated with Lord Saye and Sele as to the plausibility of the supposition; remarking at the same time as I would now, that although it was of course quite impossible to award the immortal bard great credit for chronological accuracy, it must, I thought, be admitted, that so marvellous an invention, unless really in existence, could not by any possibility of conception have been conjured up even to supply the unlimited necessities of the poet's strain. His Lordship, however, at once terminated the probability of this mill taking the precedence, even of Sir John Spielman's, by informing me that the first nobleman succeeding to that title who had property in Oxfordshire, which he acquired by marriage, was the *son* of the first Lord Say, to whom Shakspeare makes reference.

The earliest trace of the manufacture in this

country occurs in a book printed by Caxton, about the year 1490, in which it is said of John Tate—

"Which late hathe in England doo make thys paper thynne,
That now in our Englyssh thys booke is prynted inne."

His mill was situate at or near Stevenage, in Hertfordshire, and that it was considered worthy of especial notice is evident from an entry made in Henry the Seventh's Household Book, on the 25th of May, 1498—"For a rewarde geven at the paper-mylne, 16s. 8d." And again in 1499—"Geven in rewarde to Tate of the mylne, 6s. 8d."

Still, it appears to me far less probable that Shakspeare alluded to this mill, although established at a period corresponding in many respects with that of occurrences referred to in connection, than to that of Sir John Spielman's, which, standing as it did in the immediate neighbourhood of Jack Cade's rebellion, and being esteemed so important at the time, as to call forth the marked patronage of Queen Elizabeth; while the extent of the operations carried on there, if we may judge from the remarks of a poet of the time, were equally calculated to arouse undivided national interest; one can hardly help thinking, that the prominence to which Shakspeare assigns the existence of a paper mill, coupled as

such allusion is with an acknowledged liberty, in-
herent in him, of transposing events, to add force
to his style, as also with very considerable doubt
as to the exact year in which he wrote the play,
that the reference made was to none other than
that of Sir John Spielman's establishment of
1588, concerning which we find it said—

> " Six hundred men are set to work by him,
> That else might starve or seek abroad their bread,
> Who now live well, and go full brave and trim,
> And who may boast they are with paper fed."

Be the introduction or establishment of the
invention, so far as this country is concerned,
when it may; little progress appears to have resulted therefrom, even so late as the middle of
the 17th century.   In 1695, a company was
formed in Scotland "for manufacturing white
writing and printing paper," relating to which,
" Articles concluded and agreed upon at a general
meeting at Edinburgh, the 19th day of August,"
in the same year, may still be seen by those who
are sufficiently curious, in the Library of the
British Museum.   It is also recorded in the
Craftsman (910), that William the Third granted
the Huguenots refuged in England a patent for
establishing paper manufactories, and that Par_
liament likewise granted to them other privileges,
amongst which, in all probability, that very un-

satisfactory practice of putting up each ream
with two quires composed entirely of sheets
spoiled in course of production. Their under-
taking, however, like that of many others, appears to have met with very little success.

In fact, the making of paper here scarcely
reached any high degree of perfection until about
1760-5, at which period the celebrated James
Whatman established his reputation at Maidstone.

The report of the Juries of the Great Exhibition of 1851—a work from whence information
might very naturally be sought, and which
one would have supposed to be unexceptionable
in point of authenticity,—contains, I regret to say,
a very unfortunate misstatement with reference
to the position of Mr. Whatman at that time. It
is there stated that he gained his knowledge of
the manufacture prior to establishing these well-
known mills " by working as a journeyman in
most of the principal paper manufactories of the
Continent," which is altogether an erroneous assertion; for Mr. Whatman previously to his being
engaged as a manufacturer, was an officer in the
Kent Militia, and acquired the information, which
eventually rendered him so successful, by travelling in the suite of the British Ambassador to
Holland, where the best papers were then made,
and the insight thus obtained enabled his genius

to effect the great improvements afterwards so universally admitted.

At the present time, Whatman's papers (so called) are manufactured at two mills, totally distinct, both of which are still worked by the descendants of Mr. Whatman's successors; the paper in the one case being readily distinguished by the water mark, "J. Whatman, Turkey Mill," and in the other, by the water mark simply "J. Whatman," but bearing upon the upper wrapper of each ream the original and well-known stamp, containing the initials L. V. G., which are those of L. V. Gerrevink, as celebrated a Dutch manufacturer prior to Mr. Whatman's improvements, as Mr. Whatman's name has since become in all parts of the world.

In making so marked an allusion to this particular manufacture, I am bound, perhaps, to qualify it in some measure by directing attention to the comparatively recent application of continuous or rotatory motion which has, indeed, effected no more wonderful or extraordinary results than in the singular conversion of pulp into paper.

The largest paper now made by hand, which is termed Antiquarian, measures 53 inches by 31, and so great is the weight of liquid pulp employed in the formation of a single sheet, that no fewer than nine men are required, besides additional assistance in raising the mould out of the vat by means of pulleys ; while by the aid of the *paper machine*, the most perfect production may be ensured, of a continuous length, and eight feet wide, without any positive necessity for personal superintendence.

The principle of paper making by machinery is simply this, instead of employing moulds and felts of limited dimensions, as was originally the practice, the peculiar merit of the invention consists in the adaptation of an endless wire gauze to receive the paper pulp, and again an endless felt, to which in progress the paper is transferred; and thus by a marvellously delicate adjustment, while the wire at one end receives but a constant flow of liquid pulp, in the course of two or three minutes we may have, carefully wound on a roller at the other extremity, the most beautiful and serviceable of fabrics. Instead of counting sheets in course of production as formerly, or even measuring the length by yards, we may actually have the paper drawn out as it were, and wound up, miles in length. In the recent Dublin Exhibition, a sheet was exhibited which was said to have been of sufficient length to wrap round the world; but, I must confess, that I am not in a position to vouch for the accuracy of the statement. An anecdote,

however, is told, (the truth of which I have no
no reason to doubt,) of the patentee of this machine, and a relative or friend of his, of some
considerable standing and influence in the pottery
district, who were dining together about the period at which this machine was first adopted;
when the one speaking of the advantages which
he conceived the new mode would prove to his
friend, alluded above all others to the remarkable capability which it possessed of producing
paper of any length that could possibly be required. "Well," said his friend, "I very much
doubt that, but if you can make me *five miles* of
the quality I require, I shall certainly have little
hesitation in admitting all the perfection and
suitability which you have laboured to impress
upon me." The very next day the machine was
set to work, and timed, in order to ascertain
the required length wound upon the reel, which,
after being charged with Excise duty, was forwarded without delay to its destination; and, as
may be conceived, to the utter astonishment of
his incredulous friend.

It is a fact, which certainly deserves to be noticed for its singularity as well as for the strong
point of view in which it places the merits of this
invention, that an art of such great importance
to society as that of the manufacture of paper,

should have remained for at least eight centuries
since paper is first believed to have been in use,
and that upwards of 200 of those years should
have elapsed since its first introduction into England, without any mechanical improvement whatever as regards the processes which were then
employed. It is true, that various attempts from
time to time were made, but in every instance
they appear to have met with very little success.   In France, an ingenious artist contrived
three figures in wood to do the work of the vatman, the coucher, and the layer; but, after per-
severing for six months, and incurring considerable expense, he was at length compelled to
abandon his scheme.   And although paper was
previously manufactured in China, in Persia, and
indeed throughout all Asia, sometimes of considerable length, I might mention that it was so,
not by machinery, but by means of a mould of
the size of the paper intended to be made, suspended like a swing, and having men placed at
the distance of about every four feet, for the purpose of producing an uniform shaking motion,
after the mould had been immersed in the vat,
in order to compact the pulp.

Such then was the rude state of this important
manufacture, even up to the commencement of
the present century, when another ingenious

Frenchman, named Didot, brought over to this country a small model of a continuous machine, with the view of getting the benefit of English capital and mechanical skill to bring it into an operative state; and fortunately for the vigorous development of this embryo project, which had proved an abortion in France, he communicated his ideas of the practicability of the measure to a mercantile firm of considerable opulence, who, with great public spirit, at once concluded an agreement with him for the purchase of a principle which might be said at that period never to have been tried. The firm alluded to was that of the Messrs. Fourdrinier, who at that time, and for several years afterwards, were the principal stationers and paper manufacturers in Great Britain.

In order to accomplish the arduous object which those gentlemen then had in view, they appear to have laboured without intermission for nearly six years, when, after incurring an expense which would have exhausted any fortune of moderate extent (upwards of £60,000), they at length succeeded in giving some sort of organization and connection to the mechanical parts, for which they obtained a patent, and finding eventually that there was little prospect of being recompensed for labour and risk, or even reimbursed their expenses, unless Parliament should think proper to grant an extension of their patent, they determined upon making a fresh application to the Legislature for that purpose. But, it would appear that although in the Bill as it passed the House of Commons, such prolonged period extended to fourteen years; in the Lords it was limited to seven, with an understanding that such term should be extended to seven years more in the event of the patentees proving, upon a future application, that they had not been sufficiently remunerated. No such application, however, was made, in consequence of a Standing Order of the House of Lords, placed on their journal subsequently to the passing of the said act; which regulation had the effect of depriving the Messrs. Fourdrinier of any benefit whatever from the invention; and ultimately, so great were the difficulties they had to encounter, and so little encouragement or support did they receive, that the time and attention required to mature this valuable invention, and the large capital which it absorbed, were the means of reducing that wealthy and liberal firm to the humiliating condition of bankruptcy; and only within the past few months the surviving partner, Mr. Henry Fourdrinier, to whom mainly we owe the success of the invention, and as unquestionably our present high position in the scale of nations, was carried to his grave, in his ninetieth year, comparatively a beggar. A leading article in the *Times*, June 17, 1847, speaking of Mr. Henry Fourdrinier, thus concludes by advocating his claims:—" Three days only are past since an assembly, illustrious for rank and station, met to celebrate and immortalize the memory of Caxton. What more fitting or graceful opportunity of paying a tribute of respéct and justice to his fellow-labourer in an adjoining field? the one the father of printing, the other the inventor of a process by which the full benefits of printing have been realized to the civilized world. And in the case of Mr. Fourdrinier this advantage is found, that he can receive in person the tribute of a nation's gratitude; an octogenarian, he still lives; unlike Caxton, he is not yet a subject for posthumous honours. It is not a monument he wants, but justice. The world, no doubt, according to ancient precedent, would rather pay its tribute of admiration, if we should not rather say its debt of homage, after death. But it is fortunately in the power of the present age to point to a modern example of tardy but full reparation made to a living man, a great improvement upon the old rule, the mockery of a national funeral, and Westminster Abbey. Lord Dundonald's case will always stand as a brilliant exception to the common neglect of contemporary merit, and by his side it would be well to place, at no great interval, the man who in a humbler sphere, but better suited to an age of peace, has benefitted humanity by facilitating the diffusion of letters, and the acquisition of knowledge." Powerful and influential as is that journal, however, this worthy man was still left to combat so bitter a a reverse, without even the means of procuring comfort in his declining years.

But I am happy to say that an appeal has lately been made to that particular branch of trade so materially benefitted by the invention, the paper manufacturers, in the hope that thus a sufficient fund may be raised to furnish his surviving daughters with a competent annuity for the remainder of their days. And I sincerely hope that the results of this laudable effort may speedily prove to be as worthy the spirit of its originators, as on the part of the public generally it deserves consideration, as being supremely a national duty. For, be it remembered, that while the value and importance of such an invention to the paper maker is sufficiently clear and conclusive, from the fact of its general adoption throughout the united kingdom, by no less than 700 manufacturers (averaging, probably, twice that number of machines); so on the other hand, we surely cannot remain unmindful of its effects and benefits upon ourselves, when in contrasting the results of the paper-making-machine with the productions of a former period, we find the cost reduced to the consumer considerably more than one-half, in some instances to actually a fourth.

Thus then, it will be seen that as civilization has advanced, the facilities for recording and transmitting facts have uniformly improved and multiplied until now, instead of oral tradition, necessarily uncertain; instead of the bark and leaf, perishable or fragile; instead of the papyrus, so brittle; the parchment, so costly; the raw cotton paper, so expensive; instead of inscriptions by the unwieldy style and by the slow-paced pen, we have now a cheap, serviceable material, manufactured from the most useless of fabrics, and even from the very refuse of our clothing, which, conjointly with that art which preserves all other arts, enables us far to surpass in recording and transmitting power, even the greatest demands in the world's history.

NOTE.—Since the "proof" sheet was put into my hands, I have heard with very great satisfaction, that some interest has at length been awakened in the case of the Fourdriniers, and that a list has been commenced, headed with liberal subscriptions from his Grace the Duke of Sutherland, the Right Hon. the Earl of Harrowby, the Proprietors of *The Times, Illustrated London News*, and several leading firms connected with the Paper Trade.—R. H.

PAPER AND PAPER MAKING,

ANCIENT AND MODERN.

CHAPTER II.

On the Materials employed in the Formation of Paper—Method of Preparation—Processes of Comminution, Washing, Bleaching, etc. described—Paper-making by Hand—Paper-making Machine—Sizing Apparatus—Cutting Machine, etc. explained—General Observations on what are termed Water-Marks—Manner of effecting the same—Importance frequently attached to them—Ireland's Fabrication of the Shakspeare MSS.—Difficulty in procuring suitable Paper for the purpose—On the perfection to which Water-Marks have now attained, especially with reference to the production of Light and Shade, as seen in the New Bank Note, etc., etc.

In the present chapter it will be my object to take as general a glance at the principles of paper making, as in the former it was my endeavour to treat its history.

First then, we have to notice the nature of some of the materials employed. And although everybody is supposed to know that paper is made from rags, it may, perhaps, be excuseable to consider of what the rags themselves originally were composed. Unquestionably, the simplest definition one could give would be, fragments of worn-out clothing; and by clothing, no doubt, we all

E

sufficiently understand the dress, vesture or gar-
ments usually adopted by man. Still we have
to ask ourselves of what are these articles of clothing composed? It has been somewhat shrewdly
remarked in every instance, of a something of
which man has previously denuded something
else. At one time (as we all know) he cunningly
entraps innumerable individuals, of the fox,
weazel, and squirrel tribes, to strip them of their
warm and valuable fur. At another, he hatches
and feeds legions of caterpillars, that he may
rob them of the defensive padding which they
spin to protect their helplessness while passing
through the chrysalis state. Sometimes he
pastures the sheep for its skin and its wool,
occasionally setting so little store by the carcase
as to melt it into tallow, or burn it as fuel.
And even mother earth herself is treated with
no greater forbearance, by alternately feeding
her up with manure, and teazing and tormenting
her surface with tillage, she is coaxed and compelled to send forth a living vegetable down,
which is shorn, plucked and plundered from her
bosom, in the shape of cotton, flax, and hemp.

And all those silks, woollens, flax, hemp, and
cotton, in all their varied forms, whether as cam-
bric, lace, linen, holland, fustian, corduroy, bag-
ging, canvas, or even as cables, are or can be

used in the manufacture of paper of one kind or
another. Still, when we speak of rags, as of
necessity, they accumulate, and are gathered up
by those who make it their business to collect
them, they are very far from answering the
purposes of paper making. Rags, to the
paper-maker, are almost as various in point of
quality or distinction, as the materials which
are sought after through the influence of fashion.
Thus, the paper maker, in buying rags, requires
to know exactly of what the bulk is composed.
If he is a manufacturer of white papers, no matter whether intended for writing or printing,
silk or woollen rags, would be found altogether
useless, inasmuch, as is well known, the bleach
will fail to act upon any animal substance whatever. And although he may purchase even a
mixture in proper proportions adapted for the
quality he is in the habit of supplying, it is as
essential in the processes of preparation, that
they shall be previously separated. Cotton in
its raw state, as may be readily conceived, requires far less preparation than a strong hempen
fabric, and thus, to meet the requirements of the
paper-maker, we have rags classed under different
denominations, as for instance, besides *Fines* and
Seconds, we have *Thirds*, which are composed of
fustians, corduroy, and similar fabrics; *Stamps*

or *Prints* (as they are termed by the paper-
maker), which are coloured rags, and also innumerable foreign rags, distinguished by certain
well-known marks, indicating their various peculiarities. I might mention, however, that although by far the greater portion of the materials
employed are such as we have already alluded
to, it is not from their possessing any exclusive
suitableness—since various fibrous vegetable
substances have frequently been used, and are
indeed still successfully employed—but rather
on account of their comparatively trifling value,
arising from the limited use to which they are
otherwise applicable. The agitation of late, which
was partly-occasioned by the war, and partly by
a sudden and unprecedented demand, that there
was a great scarcity of fibrous materials fit to be
used in paper making, coupled with an advance
in the price of at least twenty per cent., and still
further heightened by the offer of £1,000 to any
one who could procure an advantageous substi-
tute, has necessarily called forth many suggestions, but, to quote the words of Dr. Forbes Royle,
" The generality of modern experimentalists
seem to be wholly unacquainted with the labours
of their predecessors, many of them commencing
improvement by repeating experiments which
had already been made, and announcing results

as new, which had long previously been ascertained." The latest suggestion of the kind, and indeed the only one worth referring to, is that which Lord Derby recently brought forward in the House of Lords. He first referred to a Bill before the other House of Parliament for incorporating a company established for the manufacture of paper from *flax straw*. Of course there is little new in this. The rags or materials already employed, are composed, as every body knows, to a very great extent, of the fibre of flax, and besides, possess this great advantage, that they have been repeatedly prepared for paper making by the numerous alkaline washings which they necessarily receive during their period of use, which, if left to the paper-maker, as would be the case with flax in its raw state, to be done all at once, (and it must *be* done before the fibre is fit for use,) would add so fearfully to the expense, as to render its adoption for printing or writing paper altogether unadvisable. However, Lord Derby proceeds—" It was proposed to employ the fibres of various plants indigenous to the West Indies, such as the plantain, the aloe, and others, which grow in vast abundance, and which were utterly valueless at the present moment. He need not say, that an immense abundance of this material could be produced; and he wished only to mention, that on one estate in Demerara no less than 160,000 plantain trees were cut down every year, the trees going to waste, as they were cut down only for the purpose of getting at the fruit; and this wasted material contained 250 tons of fibre, capable of being manufactured into paper."

Now, admitting *all* this, which Lord Derby is *reported* to have said, I can again assert that there is nothing whatever new in it. I have specimens of paper from the same materials, which were made several years ago. The cost, however, of reducing the plantain into fibre, coupled with the expense of freight, was found, and will still be found, to bring up the price so much, as to effectually exclude it from the manufacture of paper; for this simple reason, that rags, of necessity, must continue accumulating, and before it will answer the purpose of the paper-maker to employ new material—which is not so well adapted for his purpose as the old—he must be enabled to purchase it for considerably less than it would be worth in the manufacture of textile fabrics.

All that can be said as to the suitableness of fibre in general may be summed up in very few words; any vegetable fibre having a corrugated edge, which will enable it to cohere in the mass, is fit for the purposes of paper making; the

extent to which such might be applied can solely
be determined by the question of cost in its production; and hitherto, everything proposed has
been excluded, as in the case of the *plantain* or
banana, either by the cost of freight, the cost of
preparation, or the expenses combined.

To convey some idea of the number of substances which have been really tried; in the Library of the British Museum may be seen a book,
printed in low Dutch, containing upwards of sixty
specimens of paper, made of different materials,
the result of one man's experiments *alone*, so
far back as the year 1772. In fact, almost every
species of tough fibrous vegetable, and even animal substance, has at one time or another been
employed: even the roots of trees, their bark,
the bine of hops, the tendrils of the vine, the
stalks of the nettle, the common thistle, the stem
of the hollyhock, the sugar cane, cabbage stalks,
wood shavings, saw dust, hay, straw, willow, and
the like.

At the present time straw is occasionally used,
sometimes in connection with other materials,
such as linen or cotton rags, and even with
considerable advantage, providing the processes
of preparation are thoroughly understood.
Where such is not the case, and the silica contained in the straw has not been destroyed (by

means of a strong alkali), the paper will invariably be found more or less brittle; in some cases so much so as to be hardly applicable to any purpose whatever of practical utility. Specimens, numbered 18 and 19, affixed at the end of this work, are manufactured from as much as 80 per cent. *straw* and 20 per cent. *rope*, and certainly, as regards toughness, are excellent. No. 20, is manufactured almost entirely from *wheat straw*, which is first bleached to the utmost, and then blued by an admixture of ultramarine. The waste, however, which the straw undergoes, in addition to a most expensive process of preparation, necessarily precludes its adoption to any great extent.

An ingenious invention has recently been patented for converting large blocks of wood into paper pulp; but to what extent it is likely to receive favourable attention at the hands of paper makers generally, is quite impossible to say. The invention is very simple, consisting merely of a wooden box enclosing a grindstone, which has a roughened surface, and against which the blocks of wood are kept in close contact by a lever, a small stream of water being allowed to flow upon the stone as it turns, in order to free it of the pulp, and to assist in carrying it off through an outlet at the bottom. Of course, it is not expected, that the pulp thus produced should be employed for any but the coarser kinds of paper, in the manufacture of which there has hitherto been found the greatest scarcity of material. For all writing and printing purposes, which manifestly are the most important, nothing has yet been discovered, to lessen the value of rags, neither is it at all probable that there will be; indeed, the value of paper for some time past has considerably declined, while during the most exciting period of last year, the scarcity so much talked of, was, in fact, comparatively trifling.

The annual consumption of rags in this country alone far exceeds 120,000 tons, three-fourths of which are imported, Italy and Germany furnishing the principal supplies. That the condition in which the rags are imported furnishes any criterion of the national habits of the people from which they came, as has been frequently asserted, however plausible in theory, must, at least, be received with caution. But that is by no means important. The specimen of printing-paper, No. 21, was manufactured from a selection far from cleanly; in fact, there was not a white rag employed, while even fustians, corduroy, and coloured rags formed a considerable proportion.

In considering the various processes or stages

of the manufacture of paper, we have first to
notice that, of carefully sorting and cutting the
rags into small pieces, which is done by women;
each woman standing at a table frame, the
upper surface of which consists of very coarse
wire cloth; a large knife being fixed in the
centre of the table, nearly in a vertical position.
The woman stands so as to have the back of
the blade opposite to her, while at her right
hand on the floor is a large wooden box, with
several divisions. Her business consists in ex-
amining the rags, opening the seams, removing
dirt, pins, needles, and buttons, of endless variety,
which would be liable to injure the machinery,
or damage the quality of the paper. She then
cuts the rags into small pieces, not exceeding
four inches square, by drawing them sharply
across the edge of the knife, at the same time
keeping each quality distinct, in the several divisions of the box placed on her right hand.
During this process, much of the dirt, sand, and
so forth, passes through the wire cloth into a
drawer underneath, which is occasionally cleaned
out. After this, the rags are removed to what
is called the *dusting machine*, which is a
large cylindrical frame, covered with similar
coarse iron wire-cloth, and having a powerful
revolving shaft extending through the interior,

with a number of spokes fixed transversely, nearly long enough to touch the cage. By means of this contrivance, the machine being fixed upon an incline of some inches to the foot, the rags, which are put in at the top, have any remaining particles of dust that may still adhere to them effectually beaten out, by the time they reach the bottom.

Some objection, however, may be made to this method, which has a tendency to blow away at the same time a considerable portion of fibre set loose in cutting the rags, along with the dust. To avoid this waste, an invention has recently been brought out by a son of the late eminent Mr. Fourdrinier, which he terms his "Patent Accelerator." The process adopted is simply that of placing the rags in their dirty state in water, and employing that as a medium for carrying off the dust and dirt, in preference to air. The invention has not yet been very extensively used, and consequently I am not in a position to say much as to its merits.

The rags being thus far cleansed, have next to be boiled in an alkaline ley or solution, made more or less strong, as the rags are more or less coloured, the object being to get rid of the remaining dirt and some of the colouring matter. The proportion is from four to ten pounds of carbonate of soda with one-third of quick lime to the hundred weight of material. In this the rags are boiled for several hours, according to their quality.

The mode now adopted as the most recent improvement is that of placing the rags in large cylinders, which are constantly, though slowly, revolving, thus causing the rags to be as frequently turned over, and into which a jet of steam is cast with a pressure of something near 30 lbs. to the square inch.

After this process of cleansing, the rags are considered in a fit state to be torn or macerated until they become reduced to pulp, which was accomplished some five and thirty or forty years since, by setting them to heat and ferment for many days in close vessels, whereby in reality they underwent a species of putrefaction. Another method subsequently employed was that of beating them by means of stamping·rods, shod with iron, working in strong oak or stone mortars, and moved by water-wheel machinery. So rude and ineffective however was this apparatus, that no fewer than forty pairs of stamps were required to operate a night and a day in preparing one hundred weight of material. At the present time, the average weekly consumption of rags, at many paper mills, exceeds even 30 tons.

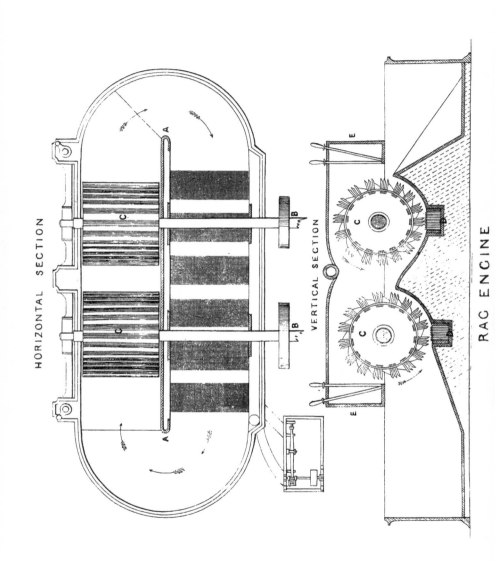

HORIZONTAL SECTION

VERTICAL SECTION

RAG ENGINE

The cylinder or engine mode of comminuting rags into paper pulp appears to have been invented in Holland, about the middle of the last century, but received very little attention here for some years afterwards. The accompanying drawing will serve to convey some idea of the wonderful rapidity with which the work is at present accomplished. No less than *twelve tons* per week can now be prepared by means of this simple contrivance. The horizontal section represents an oblong cistern, of cast iron, or wood lined with lead, into which the rags, with a sufficient quantity of water, are received. It is divided by a partition, as shown (A), to regulate the course of the stuff. The spindle upon which each cylinder (c) moves, extending across the engine, and being put in motion by a band wheel or pinion at the point (B). One cylinder, is made to traverse at a much swifter rate than the other, in order that the rags may be the more effectually triturated. The cylinders (c), as shown in the vertical section, are furnished with numerous cutters, running parallel to the axis, and again beneath them similar cutters are mounted (D) somewhat obliquely, against which, when in motion, the rags are drawn by the rapid rotation of the cylinders, and thus reduced to the smallest filaments requisite, sometimes not exceeding the sixteenth of an inch in length; the distance between the fixed and moveable blades being capable of any adjustment, simply by elevating or depressing the bearings upon which the necks of the shaft are supported. When in operation, it is of course necessary to enclose the cylinders in a case, as shown (E), otherwise a large proportion of the rags would inevitably be thrown out of the engine. I should mention, that the rags are first worked coarsely, with a stream of water running through the engine, which tends effectually to wash them, as also to open their fibres; and in order to carry off the dirty water, what is termed a *washing drum* is usually employed, consisting simply of a framework covered with very fine wire gauze, in the interior of which, connected with the shaft or spindle, which is hollow, are two suction tubes, and by this means, on the principle of a syphon, the dirty water constantly flows away through a larger tube running down outside, which is connected with that in the centre, without carrying away any of the fibre.

After this, the mass is placed in another engine, where, if necessary, it is bleached by an admixture of chloride of lime, which is retained in the engine until its action becomes apparent. The pulp is then let down into large slate cisterns to steep, prior to being reduced to a suitable consistency by the beating engine, as already described. The rolls or cylinders, however, of the beating engine are always made to rotate much faster than when employed in washing or bleaching, revolving probably from 120 to 150 times per minute, and thus, supposing the cylinders to contain 48 teeth each, passing over eight others, as shown in the drawing, effecting no fewer than 103,680 cuts in that short period. From this the great advantage of the modern engine over the old fashioned mortar machine, in turning out a quantity of paper pulp, will be at once apparent.

The operation of paper making, after the rags or materials to be used have been thus reduced and prepared, may be divided into two kinds; that which is carried on in hand-mills, where the formation of the sheet is performed by manual labour; and that which is carried on in machine-mills, where the paper is produced upon the machine wire-cloth in one continuous web.

With respect to hand-made papers, the sheet is formed by the vatman's dipping a mould of fine wire cloth fixed upon a wooden frame, and having what is termed a deckle, to determine the size of the sheet, into a quantity of pulp which has been previously mixed with water to a requisite consistency; when after gently shaking it to and fro in a horizontal position, the fibres become so connected as to form one uniform fabric, while the water drains away. The deckle is then removed from the mould, and the sheet of paper turned off upon a felt, in a pile with many others, a felt intervening between each sheet, and the whole subjected to great pressure, in order to displace the superfluous water; when after being dried and pressed without the felts, the sheets are dipped into a tub of fine animal size, the superfluity of which is again forced out by another pressing; each sheet after being finally dried, undergoing careful examination before it is finished.

Specimens 2, 3, 4, and 5, inserted at the end of the work, serve to illustrate the different stages of the manufacture. First, we have what is termed the *water-leaf*, (2) or the condition in which the paper appears after being pressed between the felts—this is the first stage. Next, a sheet from the bulk, as pressed without the felts (3) which still remains in a state unfit for writing on, not having been sized—and is in fact but white blotting paper. Then we have a sheet after sizing, which completely changes its character (4); and lastly one with the beautiful surface, which most of us, in this steel-pen age are capable of appreciating(5). This is produced by placing the sheets separately between very smooth copper plates, and then passing them through rollers, which impart a pressure of from 20 to 30 tons. After only three or four such pressures, it is simply called rolled (5), but if passed through more frequently, the paper acquires a higher surface, and is then called glazed (6).

The paper-making machine (see frontispiece) is constructed to imitate in a great measure, and in some respects to improve, the processes used in making paper by hand; but its chief advantages are the increased rapidity with which it accomplishes the manufacture, and the means of producing paper of any size which can practically be required.

By the agency of this admirable contrivance, which is so adjusted as to produce the intended effect with unerring precision, a process, which in the old system of paper-making, occupied about three *weeks*, is now performed in as many *minutes*.

The paper-making machine is supplied from the " chest " or reservoir (F), into which the pulp descends from the beating-engine, when sufficiently ground; being kept in constant motion, as it descends, by means of the agitator (G), in order that it shall not settle. From this reservoir the pulp is again conveyed by a pipe

F

into what is technically termed the "lifter" (H), which consists of a cast-iron wheel, enclosed in a wooden case, and having a number of buckets affixed to its circumference. The trough (I), placed immediately beneath the endless wire (K) is for the purpose of receiving the water which drains away from the pulp during the process of manufacture, and as this water is frequently impregnated with certain chemicals used in connexion with paper-making, it is returned again by a conducting spout, into the " lifter," where, by the rotation of the buckets, both the pulp and back-water become again thoroughly mixed, and are together raised by the lifter through the spout (L) into the vat (M) where the pulp is strained by means of a sieve or " knotter," as it is called, which is usually formed of brass, having fine slits cut in it to allow the comminuted pulp to pass through, while it retains all lumps and knots ; and so fine are these openings, in order to free the pulp entirely from anything which would be liable to damage the quality of the paper, that it becomes necessary to apply a means of exhaustion underneath, in order to facilitate the passage of the pulp through the strainer.

I have frequently examined a mass of these lumps collected upon the top of the knotter, more

particularly when printing papers are being manufactured, and have generally found them composed, to a very great extent, of India Rubber,
which is a source of much greater annoyance to
the paper maker than is readily conceived. For,
in the first place, it is next to impossible in
sorting and cutting the rags to free them entirely
from the braiding, and so forth, with which ladies
will insist upon adorning their dresses, and in the
next, the bleach failing to act upon a substance of
that character, the quality of the paper becomes
greatly deteriorated, by the large black specks
which it occasions, and which, by the combined
heat and pressure of the rolls and cylinders,
enlarge considerably as it proceeds.

Passing from this strainer the pulp is next made
to distribute itself equally throughout the entire
width of the machine, and is afterwards allowed
to flow over a small lip or ledge, in a regular and
even stream, whence it is received by the
upper surface of the endless wire (κ), upon which
the first process of manufacture takes place. Of
course the thickness of the paper depends in
some measure upon the speed at which the machine is made to travel, but it is mainly determined by the quantity of pulp allowed to flow
upon the wire, which by various contrivances
can be regulated to great nicety. Among

the specimens at the end, you will find one, No. 7,
which was made by this machine, and which is
considerably less than the thousandth of an inch
in thickness,—a thousand sheets measuring but
three quarters of an inch. And I would call your
attention to the fact, that although so thin, it is
capable of being coloured, it is capable of being
glazed, it is capable of receiving a water-mark;
and what is perhaps still more astonishing, a strip
not exceeding four inches in width, will be found
capable of sustaining a weight of twenty pounds:
so great is its tenacity.

But, to return to the machine itself. The
quantity of pulp required to flow from the vat (m)
being determined; it is first received by the continuous woven wire (k), upon which it forms itself
into paper. This wire gauze, which resembles a
jack-towel, passing over the small copper rollers
(n), round the larger one marked (o), and being
kept in proper tension by two others placed underneath. A gentle vibratory motion from side
to side is given to the wire, which assists to
spread the pulp evenly, and also to facilitate the
separation of the water, and by this means, aided
by a suction pump, the pulp solidifies as it advances. The two black squares on either side of
the "dandy" roller (p) indicate the position of
two wooden boxes, from which the air is partially

exhausted, thus causing the atmospheric pressure to operate in compacting the pulp into paper, the water and moisture being drawn through the wire, and the pulp retained on the surface.

Next, we have to notice the deckle or boundary straps (Q) which regulate the width of the paper, travelling at the same rate as the wire, and thus limiting the spread of pulp. The "dandy" roller (P), is employed to give any impression to the paper that may be required. We may suppose for instance, that the circumference of that roller answers exactly to the length or breadth of the wire forming a hand mould, which, supposing such wire to be fixed or curved in that form, would necessarily leave the same impression as when employed in the ordinary way. Being placed between the air boxes, the paper becomes impressed by it when in a half formed state, and whatever marks are thus made, the paper will effectually retain. The marks seen in Specimens 2, 3, 4, and 5, have been occasioned by a hand mould, those in 6, 7, 9, and 11, are impressions given by a dandy roller. The two rollers following the dandy, marked (R) and (O), are termed couching rollers, from their performing a similar operation in the manufacture of machine-made papers, to the business of the coucher in conducting the process by hand. They are simply wooden rollers covered with felt. In some instances, however,

the upper couch roll (R) is made to answer
a double purpose. In making writing or other
papers, where smalts, ultramarine, and various
colours are used, considerable difference will
frequently be found in the tint of the paper when
the two sides are compared, in consequence of
the colouring matter sinking to the lower side,
by the natural subsidence of the water, or from
the action of the suction boxes; and to obviate
this, instead of employing the ordinary couch
roll, which acts upon the *upper* surface of the
paper, a hollow one is substituted, having a
suction box within it, acted upon by an air pump,
which tends in some measure to counteract the
effect, justly considered objectionable. Merging
from those rollers the paper is received from the
wire gauze by a continuous felt (s), which conducts
it through two pair of pressing rollers, and afterwards to the drying cylinders. You will observe,
that the paper, after passing through the first
pair of rollers, is carried along the felt for some
distance, and then turned over, in order to
receive a corresponding pressure on the other
side, thus obviating the inequality of surface
which would otherwise be apparent, especially if
the paper were to be employed for books.

The advantage gained by the use of so great a
length of felt, is simply, that it becomes less necessary to stop the machine for the purpose of

washing it, than would be the case if the felt were limited in length to its absolute necessity.

In some instances, when the paper being made is sized in the pulp with such an ingredient as *resin*, the felt becomes so completely clogged in the space of a few hours, that unless a very great and apparently unnecessary length of felt be employed, a considerable waste of time is constantly incurred in washing or changing the felt. To obviate all this—whether waste of time or waste of felt—I have suggested in one or two quarters, the propriety of passing the felt, as it returns from conducting the paper to the heated cylinders, through a trough of water, and while travelling through the water to apply suction boxes to both the upper and lower surface of the felt, which by an alternate action, might be made sufficiently powerful to remove all impurity, without in any way obstructing the progress of the felt; which if found necessary, might be assisted, while at the same time the felt would be restored to its original condition, by employing a suction *roller* to which a steady motion was given in connexion with the machine.

The operation of the manufacture will now be apparent. The pulp flowing from the reservoir into the lifter, and thence through the strainer, passes over a small lip to the continuous wire, being there partially com-

pacted by the shaking motion, more thoroughly
so on its passage over the air boxes, receiving
any desired marks by means of the dandy roller
passing over the continuous felt between the first
pressing rollers, then turned over to receive a
corresponding pressure on the other side, and
from thence off to the drying cylinders, which
are heated more or less by injected steam; the
cylinder which receives the paper first, being
heated less than the second, the second than the
third, and so on; the paper after passing over
those cylinders, being finally wound upon a reel,
as shown, unless it be printing paper, which can
be sized sufficiently in the pulp, by an admixture
of alum, soda, and resin, or the like; in which
case it may be at once conducted to the cutting
machine, to be divided into any length and width
required.   But, supposing it to be intended for
writing purposes, it has first to undergo a more
effectual method of sizing, as shown in the accompanying drawing.   The size in this instance
being made from parings obtained from tanners,
curriers, and parchment-makers, as employed in
the case of hand-made papers.   Of course, sizing
in the pulp or in the engine offers many advantages, but as gelatine, or animal size, which is
really essential for all good writing qualities,
cannot at present be employed during the process of manufacturing by the machine without

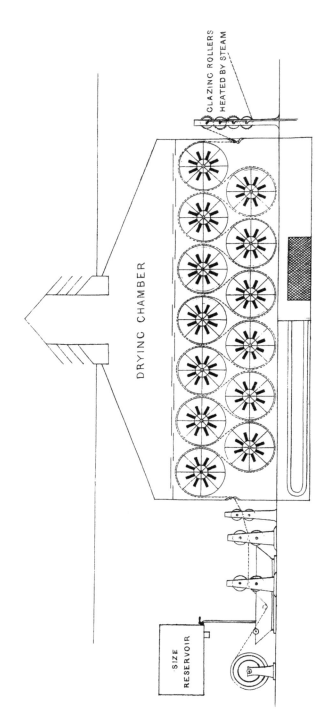

GLAZING ROLLERS
HEATED BY STEAM

DRYING CHAMBER

SIZE
RESERVOIR

SIZING APPARATUS

injury to the felts, it becomes necessary to pass the web of paper, after it has been dried by the cylinders, through this apparatus.

In most cases, however, the paper is at once guided as it issues from the machine, through the tub of size, and is thence carried over the skeleton drums shown, inside each of which are a number of fans rapidly revolving; sometimes there are forty or fifty of these drums in succession, the whole confined in a chamber heated by steam. I have seen a paper-machine with the sizing apparatus attached, which from the wire-cloth where the pulp first flows on, to the cutting machine at the extremity, measured no less than one thousand feet. The advantage of drying the paper in this manner over so many of these drums is, that it turns out much harder and stronger, than if dried more rapidly over heated cylinders. Some manufacturers adopt a peculiar process of sizing, which in fact answers very much better, and is alike applicable to papers made by hand or by machine, provided the latter description be first cut into pieces or sheets of the required dimensions. The contrivance consists of two revolving felts, between which the sheets are carried under several rollers through a long trough of size, being afterwards hung up to dry upon

lines, previously to rolling or glazing. The paper
thus sized becomes much harder and stronger,
by reason of the freedom with which the sheets
can contract in drying; and this is mainly the
reason why paper made by hand continues to be
so much tougher than that made by the machine,
in consequence of the natural tendency of the pulp
to contract in drying, and consequently becoming,
where no resistance is offered, more entwined or
entangled, which of course adds very considerably
to the strength and durability of the paper.
In making by the machine, this tendency, you
will observe, is completely checked.

The next operation which we have to notice,
now that the paper is finished, is that of cutting
it into standard sizes. Originally, the reel upon
which it was finally wound, was formed so that
its diameter might be lessened or increased at
pleasure, according to the sizes which were required. Thus, for instance, supposing we wanted
to cut the web of paper into sheets of 18 inches
in length, we should either lessen the diameter
of the reel to 6 inches, and thus the circumference to 18 inches, or if convenient increase it to
36 inches, afterwards cutting the paper in two
with a large knife, similar in size and shape
to that employed by a cheesemonger; the width
of the web being regulated by the deckle straps

(Q) to either twice or three times the width of the sheet, as the case might be. However, in regard to the length considerable waste, of necessity, arose, from the great increase in the circumference of the reel as the paper was wound upon it, and to remedy this, several contrivances have been invented. To dwell upon their various peculiarities or separate stages of improvement, would, no doubt, prove to the general reader of little comparative interest, I shall, therefore, confine my attention to a brief explanation of the cutting machine, of which I have given an illustration, and which is unquestionably the best, as well as the most ingenious, invention of the kind.

The first movement or operation peculiar to this machine is that of cutting the web of paper longitudinally, into such widths as may be required. And this is effected by means of circular blades, placed at stated distances, which receive the paper as it issues direct from the other machinery, and by a very swift motion, much greater than that at which the paper travels, slit it up with unerring precision wherever they may be fixed.

A pair of those circular blades is shown in the drawing (a), the upper one being much larger than the lower, which is essential to the smoothness of the cut. And not only is the upper blade larger in circumference, but it is also made to revolve with much greater rapidity, by means of employing a small pinion, worked by one at least twice its diameter, which is fixed upon the same shaft as the lower blade, to which the motive power is applied. The action aimed at is precisely such as we obtain from a pair of scissors.

The web, as it is termed by the paper-maker, being thus severed longitudinally, the next operation is that of cutting it off into sheets of some particular length horizontally; and to do this requires a most ingenious movement. To give a very general idea of the contrivance, the dotted line is intended to represent the paper travelling on with a rapidity in some cases of 80 feet per minute, and yet its course has to be temporarily arrested while the required separation is effected, and that too without the paper's accumulating in any mass, or getting creased in the slightest degree.

The large drum (b), over which the paper passes, in the direction indicated by the arrows, has simply an alternating motion, which serves to gather the paper in such lengths as may be required. The crank arm (c), which is capable of any adjustment either at top or bottom, regulating the extent of the movement backwards and forwards, and thus the length of the sheet. As soon as the paper to be cut off has

CUTTING MACHINE

passed below the point (*d*), at which a *presser* is suspended, having an alternating motion given to it, in order to make it approach to, and recede from, a stationary presser-board; it is taken hold of as it descends from the drum, and the length pendant from the presser, is instantly cut off by the moveable knife (*e*), to which motion is given by the crank (*f*), the connecting rod (*g*), the lever (*h*), and the connecting rod (*i*). The combined motion of these rods and levers, admits of the moveable knife (*e*), remaining nearly quiescent for a given time, and then speedily closing upon the fixed knife (*k*), cutting off the paper in a similar manner to a pair of shears, when it immediately slides down a board, or in some instances is carried along a revolving felt, at the extremity of which several men or boys are placed to receive the sheets, according to the number into which the width of the web is divided.

As soon as the pressers are closed for a length of paper to be cut off, the motion of the gathering drum is reversed, smoothing out the paper upon its surface, which is now held between the pressers; the tension roll (*l*), taking up the slack in the paper as it accumulates, or ratherb earing it gently down, until the movement of the drum is again reversed to furnish another

length.   The handle (*m*), is employed merely to
stop a portion of the machinery, should the
water-mark not fall exactly in the centre of the
sheet, when by this means it can be momentarily
adjusted.

The paper being thus made, and cut up into
sheets of stated dimensions, is next looked over
and counted out into quires of 24 sheets, and
afterwards into reams of 20 quires; which subsequently, under the superintendence of an Excise
Officer, are carefully weighed and stamped, previously to their being sent into the market.

Connected with the manufacture of paper,
there is one point of considerable interest and
importance, and that is, what is commonly, but
erroneously, termed the *water-mark*, which may
be noticed in the Times Newspaper, in the New
Bank of England Notes, Cheques and Bills, as
also in every Postage and Receipt Label of the
present day.

The curious, and in some instances absurd
terms, which now puzzle us so much in describing the different sorts and sizes of paper, may
frequently be explained by reference to the
various paper marks which have been adopted
at different periods.   In ancient times, when
comparatively few people could read, pictures of
every kind were much in use where writing

would now be employed. Every shop, for
instance, had its sign, as well as every public-
house, and those signs were not then, as they
often are now, only painted upon a board,
but were invariably actual models of the thing
which the sign expressed—as we still occasionally
see some such sign as a bee-hive, a tea-canister,
or a doll, and the like. For the same reason
printers employed some device, which they put
upon the title pages and at the end of their
books, and paper makers also introduced marks,
by way of distinguishing the paper of their manufacture from that of others; which marks
becoming common, naturally gave their names
to different sorts of paper. And since names
often remain long after the origin of them is
forgotten and circumstances are changed, it is
not surprising to find the old names still in use,
though in some cases they are not applied to
the same things which they originally denoted.
One of the illustrations of ancient water-mark
which I have given in the accompanying plate;
that of an open hand with a star at the top,
which was in use as early as 1530; probably
gave the name to what is still called *hand*
paper.

Another very favourite paper-mark, at a subsequent period 1540-60, was the jug or pot,

which is also shown, and would appear to have originated the term *pot* paper. The foolscap was a later device, and does not appear to have been nearly of such long continuance as the former. It has given place to the figure of Britannia, or that of a lion rampant, supporting the cap of liberty on a pole. The name, however, has continued, and we still denominate paper of a particular size, by the title of *foolscap*. The original figure has the cap and bells, of which we so often read in old plays and histories, as the particular head-dress of the fool, who at one time formed part of every great man's establishment.

I have met with the water-mark of a cap, much simpler than that which we have just noticed, somewhat resembling the jockey-caps of the present day, with a trifling ornamentation or addition to the upper part. The first edition of " Shakspeare," printed by *Isaac Jaggard & Ed. Blount,* 1623, will be found to contain this mark, interspersed with several others of a different character. No doubt the general use of the term *cap* to various papers of the present day owes its origin to marks of this description.

The term *imperial* was in all probability derived from the finest specimens of papyri, which were so called by the ancients.

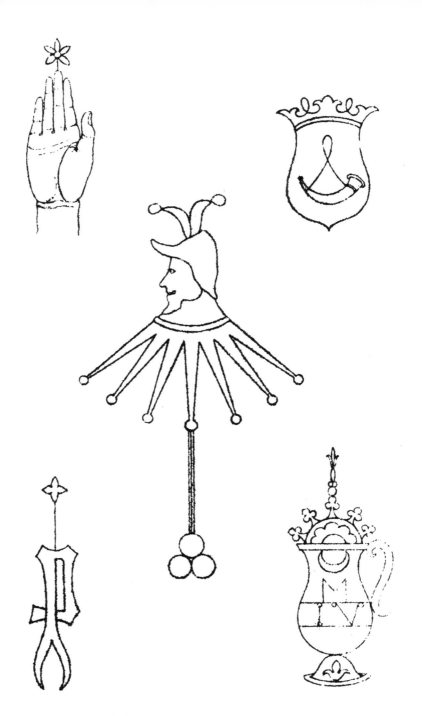

ANCIENT WATERMARKS.

Post paper seems to have derived its name from the post-horn, which at one time was its distinguishing mark. It does not appear to have been used prior to the establishment of the general post-office (1670), when it became the custom to blow a horn, to which circumstance no doubt we may attribute its introduction. The mark is still frequently used, but the same change which has so much diminished the number of painted signs in the streets of our towns and cities, has nearly made paper-marks a matter of antiquarian curiosity; the maker's name being now generally used, and the mark, in the few instances where it still remains, serving the purpose of mere ornament, rather than that of distinction.

Water-marks, however, have at various periods been the means of detecting frauds, forgeries and impositions, in our courts of law and elsewhere, to say nothing of the protection they afford in the instances already referred to, such as bank notes, cheques, receipt, bill, and postage stamps. The celebrated Curran once distinguished himself in a case which he had undertaken, by shrewdly referring to the water-mark, which effectually determined the verdict. And another instance, which I introduce merely in the form of an amusing anecdote, occurred once at Messina, where the monks of a certain monastery exhibited, with great triumph, a letter as being written by the Virgin Mary with her own hand. Unluckily for them, however, this was not, as it easily might have been, written upon the ancient papyrus, but on paper made of rags. On one occasion a visitor, to whom this was shown, observed, with affected solemnity, that the letter involved also a *miracle*, for the paper on which it was written was not in existence until several centuries after the mother of our Lord had died.

A further illustration of the kind occurs in a work entitled "Ireland's Confessions," which was published respecting his fabrication of the Shakspeare manuscripts,—a literary forgery even still more remarkable, I think, than that which is said to have been perpetrated by Chatterton, as Rowley's Poems.

The interest which at the time was universally felt in this production of Ireland's, may be partially gathered from the fact, that the whole of the original edition, which appeared in the form of a shilling pamphlet, was disposed of in a few hours ; while so great was the eagerness to obtain copies afterwards, that single impressions were sold in an auction room at the extravagant price of a guinea.

This gentleman tells us, at one part of his explanation, that the sheet of paper which he used was the outside of several others, on some of which accounts had been kept in the reign of Charles the First; and being at that time wholly unacquainted with the water-marks used in the reign of Queen Elizabeth, "I carefully selected (says he) two half-sheets, not having any mark whatever, on which I penned my first effusion." A few pages further on he writes—"Being thus urged forward to the production of more manuscripts, it became necessary that I should possess a sufficient quantity of old paper to enable me to proceed, in consequence of which I applied to a bookseller, named Verey, in Great May's Buildings, St. Martin's Lane, who, for the sum of five shillings, suffered me to take from all the folio and quarto volumes in his shop, the fly leaves which they contained. By this means I was amply stored with that commodity; nor did I fear any mention of the circumstance by Mr. Verey, whose quiet unsuspecting disposition, I was well convinced, would never lead him to make the transaction public, in addition to which he was not likely even to know anything concerning the supposed Shaksperian discovery by myself, and even if he had, I do not imagine that my purchase of the old paper in question, would

have excited in him the smallest degree of suspicion. As I was fully aware from the variety
of water-marks which are in existence at the
present day, that they must have constantly
been altered since the period of Elizabeth, and
being for some time wholly unacquainted with
the water-marks of that age, I very carefully
produced my first specimens of the writing on
such sheets of old paper as had no mark whatever. Having heard it frequently stated that
the appearance of such marks on the papers
would have greatly tended to establish their validity, I listened attentively to every remark
which was made upon the subject, and from
thence I at length gleaned the intelligence that
a jug was the prevalent water-mark of the reign
of Elizabeth, in consequence of which I inspected
all the sheets of old paper then in my possession,
and having selected such as had the jug upon
them, I produced the succeeding manuscripts
upon these, being careful, however, to mingle
with them a certain number of blank leaves, that
the production on a sudden of so many water-
marks might not excite suspicion in the breasts
of those persons who were most conversant with
the manuscripts."

Thus, this notorious literary forgery, through
the cunning ingenuity of the perpetrator, ulti-

mately proved so successful as to deceive many
learned and able critics of the age. Indeed, on
one occasion a kind of certificate was drawn up,
stating that the undersigned names were affixed
by gentlemen who entertained no doubt whatever as to the validity of the Shaksperian production, and that they voluntarily gave such
public testimony of their convictions upon the
subject. To this document several names were
appended by persons as conspicuous for their
erudition as they were pertinacious in their
opinions.

The water-mark in the form of a letter p, of
which I have given an illustration, is taken from
Caxton's well-known work, "The Game of the
Chesse," a *fac simile* of which is about to be published as a tribute to his memory. Paper has
recently been made expressly for the purpose,
in exact representation of the original, and containing this water-mark, which will be found
common in works printed by him.

The ordinary mode of effecting such paper
marks as we have been describing is that of
affixing a stout wire in the form of any object
to be represented to the surface of the fine wire-
gauze, of which the hand-mould, or machine
dandy roller is constructed.

The perfection, however, to which water-marks
have now attained, which in many instances is

really very beautiful, is owing to a more ingenious
method recently patented, and since adopted by
the Bank of England, as affording considerable
protection to the public indeterm ining the gen-
uineness of a bank note.

For the original idea of producing light and
shade, as seen in specimens 1, 13, and 15, we are
indebted to Mr. Wm. Henry Smith, whose patient
perseverance, and laborious efforts, at length
enabled him to overcome many difficulties,
and finally to produce not only any peculiarity
of design, however complicate, but also to
secure its repetition with a certainty of uni-
formity which, in the process of manufacture
as hitherto conducted, it was found impossible to
accomplish.

To produce a line water-mark of the character
shown in specimens 10, 12, and 16, or of any of the
autographs or crests in No. 14, (which sheet was
produced from the mould which I employed at
the London Institution,) we might either engrave
the pattern or device first in some yielding surface, precisely as we should engrave a copper-plate
for printing, and afterwards by immersing the
plate in a solution of sulphate of copper, and
electrotyping it in the usual way, allow the
interstices of the engraving to give it as were a
casting of pure copper, and thus an exact repre-

sentation of the original device, which, upon being removed from the plate, and affixed to the surface of the wire-gauze forming the mould, would produce a corresponding impression in the paper: or, supposing perfect identity to be essential, as in the case of a bank note, we might engrave the design upon the surface of a steel die, taking care to cut those parts in the die deepest which are intended to give greater effect in the paper, and then, after having hardened, and otherwise properly prepared the die, it would be placed under a steam hammer or other stamping apparatus, for the purpose of producing what is technically termed a " force," which is required to assist in transferring an impression from the die to a plate of sheet brass. This being done, the die, with the mould-plate in it, would next be taken to a perforating or cutting machine, where the back of the mould-plate—that is the portion which projects above the face of the die—would be removed, while that portion which was impressed into the design engraven, would remain untouched, and this being subsequently taken from the interstices of the die and placed in a frame upon a backing of fine wire-cloth, becomes a mould for the manufacture of paper of the pattern which is desired, or for the production of any water-mark, autograph, crest or device, however complicate.

Light and shade, as seen in Nos. 1, 13, and 15, are occasioned by a very similar process, but one which perhaps requires a little more care, and necessarily becomes somewhat more tedious. For instance, in the former case the pulp is distributed equally throughout the entire surface of the wire forming the mould, whereas *now* we have to contrive the means of increasing to a very great nicety the thickness or distribution of the pulp, and at the same time to make provision for the water's draining away. This has been accomplished, as in the case of No. 13, by first taking an electrotype of the raised surface of any model or design, and again from that, forming in a similar manner a matrix or mould, both of which are subsequently mounted upon lead or gutta percha, in order that they may withstand the pressure which is required to be put upon them in giving impression to a sheet of very fine copper wire-gauze, which, in the form of a mould, and in the hands of the vatman, suffices ultimately to produce such beautiful transparent effects in paper pulp as those to which I have called your attention. By similar means a portrait of the Emperor Napoleon was produced for the Paris Exhibition.

The other specimens, 1 and 15, are produced in the same manner as the word "Five" in the centre of the new Bank of England note. The deepest shadows in the water-mark being occasioned by the deepest engraving upon the die, the lightest, by the shallowest, and so forth; the die being employed to give impression by means of the stamping press and "force" to the fine wire-gauze itself, which by this means, providing the die be properly cut, is accomplished far more successfully than by any other process, and with the additional advantage of securing perfect identity.

It may be interesting to call attention to the contrast as regards the method of mould-making originally practised, and that which has recently been adopted by the Bank of England. In a pair of five pound note moulds, prepared by the old process, there were 8 curved borders, 16 figures, 168 large waves, and 240 letters, which had all to be separately secured by the finest wire to the waved surface. There were 1,056 wires, 67,584 twists, and the same repetition where the stout wires were introduced to support the under surface. Therefore, with the backing, laying, large waves, figures, letters, and borders, before a pair of moulds was completed, there were some hundreds of thousands of stitches, most of which are now avoided by the new patent. But further, by this

multitudinous stitching and sewing, the parts
were never placed precisely in the same position,
and the water-mark was consequently never
identical. Now, the same die gives impression to
the metal which transfers it to the water-mark,
with a certainty of identity unattainable before,
and one could almost say, never to be surpassed.

But, as it has been properly remarked,
may we not detect principles in this process
which are not only valuable to the Bank, but to
all public establishments having important documents on paper, for what can exceed the value of
such a test for discovering the deceptions of dishonest men. One's signature, crest, or device of
any kind, rendering the paper exclusively one's
own, can now be secured in a pair of moulds, at
the cost merely of a few guineas.

Thus then, I have endeavoured briefly to glance
at all the varied manipulations comprised in the
term Paper Making; from the soiled rags,
which by this regenerating process, are converted into pure and spotless paper, and thence to
the operations which in degree distinguish it,
until finally, the stronger the test for illumi-
nating its perfection, but suffices to prove it of
that most aristocratic class, to which belongs our
new bank note.

PAPER AND PAPER MAKING,

ANCIENT AND MODERN.

CHAPTER III.

Anecdote of an over-curious enquirer—Its probable application to many readers—Paper Making, when straightforward, extremely simple, but ordinarily involving considerable chemical and practical skill—Brief review of artificial aids—Anecdotes of the deleterious effects of bleaching, and of imparting colour to the " stuff'—Ultramarine, its use and abuse—Manufactured Paper, its varieties and peculiarities—Excise Regulations—Paper Duty—Conclusion.

Not long since I heard of a very inquisitive gentleman, as some people would term him, who wrote to a friend of mine asking him to obtain certain information respecting the manufacture of *isinglass;* and although the questions put, were by no means essential to general knowledge, my friend complied with his request, and forwarded the application to the party immediately interested in its production; who, with similar promptitude undertook to furnish the answers per return of post, upon receiving from the anxious applicant a repetition of the inquiry, accompanied by his cheque for three thousand pounds.

Now, it is not at all improbable that many into whose hands this book may fall will be disposed to charge me with similar motives, as concealing secrets connected with paper making. It is, however, a reliable fact, that nothing can be more simple or straightforward than the manufacture of that, which, for want of a more comprehensive expression, I must denominate *genuine paper*. Chemical aid, combined with great practical skill, is absolutely indispensable, I admit, to enable one to keep pace with competition in the present day; when even the rags and tatters, cast off by the very poorest of the poor, may now be forwarded after sunrise, many miles distant, and before sunset, received back again converted into a becoming groundwork for the most enchanting *billet-doux*. Still, productions of this character, when contrasted with the results of a slow and simple manipulation of finer materials, even to the unpractised eye, will be found far inferior, as regards the one grand test of superiority, viz., *durability*. The slower the process of manufacture is conducted from beginning to end, from the trituration of the "stuff" in the rag engine, to the formation of the sheet, its sizing, drying, and rolling, the stronger and more durable will the paper ultimately turn out. No. 17, which is a specimen of paper thus carefully made, and almost as tough and durable as parchment, is capable of sustaining a weight of no less than 200 lbs., simply by means of a slip the width of a bank note. If, however, we glance at the other extreme, and take the aids frequently adopted to produce paper of apparent excellence from comparatively worthless materials, we shall find occasion to regret more than one form of artificial assistance, which is perpetually liable to objection. The effects, for instance, of excessive bleaching are still occasionally manifested, although by a better system of washing the pulp and the use of counteracting chemicals, evils which at one time resulted therefrom are now mainly checked. Within the recollection of my father, it was not at all an uncommon occurrence for a parcel of paper to become so completely perished from the circumstance of its not having been thoroughly washed after bleaching, that to draw a sheet as a sample, and to fold it up in the usual way, was found utterly impossible, without the sheets being cracked or broken at every fold. · In some instances, the fibre was so completely destroyed, that an entire ream, composed of 480 sheets, might be as readily snapped asunder as a piece of rotten wood, merely by giving it a sharp blow against the back of a chair. The evils and in-

conveniences which must have resulted from
this are altogether incalculable. Mr. Hansard
("Typographia," 1825,) thus writes, "Whole
piles of quired stock, meaning books unbound,
are already crumbling to dust in the warehouses
of booksellers, never to come to light as books,
and many a volume designed to enrich the library
of its possessor and to descend as an heir-loom
to posterity, now presents to the mortified owner
its elegant print surrounded by a margin of tan
colour, which in some instances forms, as it were,
a complete frame round each page, the oil var-
nish in the composition of the ink seeming to
preserve the interstices between the print from
the same kind of discoloration. School books (he
adds) printed on this species of paper, will
scarcely last out their destined period, from one
vacation to the next." Another gentleman informs us, speaking of a quantity of Bibles, which
were printed for the British and Foreign Bible
Society, that one in his possession, printed at the
University press at Oxford in 1816, (which had
never been used) was then, within a year or two
afterwards, literally crumbling into dust. "Almost the entire book of Genesis (says he) has
mouldered away, and left not a trace behind."
Of course, paper of this description (if it deserves
the name at all) would prove very bad stock in

like manner for the stationer, being for any purpose whatever as utterly useless as it was worthless, with but one exception, which in the case of a large parcel of this description, I understand, was once adopted, viz., that of shipping it in very common cases, thus securing the drawback, which, at that time, was far more worth consideration than it would be now, and eventually consigning it to the fate of innumerable other treasures within the boundless limits of the ocean.

If to speak of the various artificial aids which the manufacturer has recourse to in the present day be necessary, it surely cannot but be equally advisable, to point out their main cause; and if blame exist at all, or fault be found, it cannot, I apprehend, be rested with greater safety than with those who, stipulating their own terms, must of necessity be supplied in their own way. The paper maker requires to be remunerated; and with competition to grapple with and contend against, not only all the improvements which mechanical science is capable of supplying, must be adopted by him, but even in many cases, however much to be regretted, he is tempted to an intermixture of noxious and heterogeneous materials, in order that the minimum price may be attained.

Some specimens of paper will be found to con-

tain as much as one-fourth their weight of gyp-
sum; and in fact, even worse material, as a
means of adulteration, is as eagerly sought after
by the manufacturer of paper, as the public generally, to the sacrifice of quality, seek the cheap-
est article which it is possible to procure. I
need but refer, as an instance, to the packing
papers of the present day, of which one sheet
properly made (25), contrasted with one of the
same weight of the sort usually selected, will be
found to possess three times the amount of
strength, although not 10 per cent. higher in price.

With a finer class of papers common materials
are as readily employed, through the assistance
of some colouring matter, which tends to conceal
the imperfection. Indeed, it would be difficult
to name an instance of apparent deception more
forcible than that which is accomplished by the
use of ultramarine. Until very recently the fine
bluish tinge given to many writing papers was
derived from the admixture of that expensive
mineral blue, the oxide of cobalt, generally
termed *smalts,* and which has still the advantage over the ultramarine of imparting a
colour which will endure for a much longer
period. One pound of ultramarine, however,
going further than four of smalts at the same
price, the former necessarily meets with more

extended application, and where the using is rightly understood, and the materials employed instead of being fine rags, comparative rubbish, excessively bleached; its application proves remarkably serviceable in concealing for a time all other irregularities, and even far surpassing in appearance the best papers of the kind.

At first the introduction of ultramarine led to some difficulty in sizing the paper, for so long as smalts continued to be used, any amount of alum might be employed, and it was actually added to the size to preserve it from putrefaction. But since artificial ultramarine is bleached by alum, it became of course necessary to add this salt to the size in very small proportions, and as a natural consequence, the gelatine was no longer protected from the action of the air, which led to incipient decomposition, and in such cases the putrefaction once commenced, proceeded even after the size was dried on the paper, and gave to it a most offensive smell, which rendered the paper unsaleable. This difficulty, however, has now been overcome, and providing the size be quite free from taint when applied to the paper, and quickly dried, putrefaction will not subsequently occur; but if decay has once commenced, it cannot be arrested by drying only.

H

The practice of blueing the paper pulp had its origin in a singularly accidental circumstance, which not merely as an historical fact, but as forming an amusing anecdote, is perhaps worth mentioning. It occurred about the year 1790, at a paper mill belonging to Mr. Buttenshaw, whose wife, on the occasion in question, was superintending the washing of some fine linen, when accidentally she dropped her bag of powdered blue into the midst of some pulp in a forward state of preparation, and so great was the fear she entertained of the mischief she had done, seeing the blue rapidly amalgamated with the pulp, that all allusion to it was studiously avoided; until, on Mr. Buttenshaw's inquiring in great astonishment what it was that had imparted the peculiar colour to the pulp, his wife, perceiving that no very great damage had been done, took courage and at once disclosed the secret, for which she was afterwards rewarded in a remarkable manner by her husband, who being naturally pleased with an advance of so much as four shillings per bundle, upon submitting the *improved* make to the London market, immediately purchased a costly scarlet cloak, (somewhat more congenial to taste in those days, it is presumed, than it would be now,) which he carefully conveyed home, and presented with much satisfaction to the sharer of his joy.

Although the practice of blueing paper is not, perhaps, so customary now as was the case a few years back, the extent to which it is still carried may be a matter of considerable astonishment. On its first introduction, when, as regards colour, the best paper was anything but pleasing, so striking a novelty would no doubt be hailed as a great improvement, and as such received into general use, but when we contrast a *first-class* paper now (8), without any colouring matter whatever, and without any superfluous marks upon its surface, with the miserable blue tints one so frequently sees, it becomes a source of surprise, that the superior delicacy of the former is not more generally appreciated.

The only objection which can be urged against the use of a colourless paper is, its comparative transparency when glazed in the ordinary way : but this is by no means essential.   A finished surface imparted by calendering, when contrasted with one more highly glazed, will be found wholly superior for a writing paper, and unobjectionable as regards opaqueness.

In paper making, there has seldom, perhaps, arisen a greater difficulty than in furnishing a supply suited to the purposes of photography. Unquestionably, great care is requisite in the selection of the materials, their preparation, and subsequent manufacture. But the difficulty is owing more to the want of positive information on the part of the photographer, than to failure in the exertions of the Paper Maker. I have recently been informed by a gentleman who has devoted much time and attention to this particular class of paper, that after forwarding specimens to many score members of that profession, and inviting observations and suggestions thereon, not one in ten favoured him with any reply, and of those who did, although many first-rate names might be mentioned, the conclusions to which they severally came were totally adverse.

It is not my intention to wander further into the field of paper and paper making than to mark the boundary which has been set up by Act of Parliament, in the form of Excise Regulations, with a few general observations upon the varieties and peculiarities of manufactured paper, as a becoming and at the present time somewhat important termination to our subject.

Manufactured paper, independently of the miscellaneous kinds, such as blotting, filtering, and the like, which are rendered absorbent by the free use of *woollen* rags, may be divided into three distinct classes, *viz.*, writing, printing, and wrapping. The former again into *five*, cream wove

(8), yellow wove (17), blue wove (7), cream laid (16), and blue laid (5). The printing into *two*, laid and wove, and the latter into *four*, blue (22), purple (24), brown (25), and whited brown (23), as it is commonly termed. Each of these sorts ought again to be classified, until it would appear as if not merely all the wants, wishes, and fancies of mankind had been fully studied and provided for, but that even the utmost bounds of variety in like manner had been included, in order to test the comprehensiveness of human caprice.

To give a simple definition of the mode adopted for distinguishing the various kinds, I must include, with the class denominated *writing* papers, those which are used for drawing, which being sized in like manner, and with the exception of one or two larger kinds, of precisely the same dimensions as those passing by the same name, which are used strictly for writing purposes, (the only distinction, in fact, being, that the drawings are cream wove, while the writings are laid,) there would of course be no necessity for separating them. Indeed, since many of the sizes used for printing are exactly the same as those which would be named as writing papers, for the sake of abridgment I will reduce my distinctions of difference to but two heads, fine and coarse; under the latter.

including the ordinary brown papers, the whited
brown, or small hand quality, and the blues and
purples, used by grocers. The smallest size of
the fine quality, as sent from the mill, measures
12½ by 15 inches, and is termed Pot; next to
that Foolscap, 17 by 13½; then Post, 18¾ by 15¼;
Copy, 20 by 16; Large Post, 20¾ by 16½; Medium
Post, 18 by 23; Sheet-and-third Foolscap, 23
by 13¼; Sheet-and-half Foolscap, 24½ by 13¼;
Double Foolscap, 27 by 17; Double Pot, 30 by
25; Double Post, 30½ by 19: Double Crown, 20
by 30; Demy, 20 by 15½; ditto Printing, 22½ by
17¾; Medium, 22 by 17½; ditto Printing, 23 by
18½; Royal, 24 by 19; ditto Printing, 25 by 20;
Super Royal, 27 by 19; ditto Printing, 21 by 27;
Imperial, 30 by 22; Elephant, 28 by 23; Atlas,
34 by 26; Columbier, 34½ by 23½; Double Elephant, 26¾ by 40; and Antiquarian, 53 by 31.
The different sizes of letter and note paper
ordinarily used are prepared from those kinds
by the stationer, whose business consists chiefly
in smoothing the edges of the paper, and afterwards packing it up in some tasteful form, which
serves to attract attention.

Under the characteristic names of coarse
papers may be mentioned Kent Cap, 21 by 18;
Bag Cap, 19½ by 24; Havon Cap, 21 by 26;
Imperial Cap, 22 by 29; Double 2-lb., 17 by 24;

Double 4-lb., 21 by 30; Double 6-lb., 19 by 28;
Casing of various dimensions, also Cartridges, with
other descriptive names, besides Middle Hand,
22 by 16; Lumber Hand, 19½ by 29; Royal Hand,
20 by 25; Double Small Hand, 19 by 29 ; and of
the purples, such significations as Copy Loaf,
16¾ by 21¾, 38-lb.; Powder Loaf, 18 by 26, 58-lb.;
Double Loaf, 16⅓ by 23, 48-lb.; Single Loaf, 21⅓
by 27, 78-lb.; Lump, 23 by 33, 100-lb.; Hambro',
16⅓ by 23, 48-lb.; Titler, 29 by 35, 120-lb.;
Prussian or Double Lump, 32 by 42, 200-lb.; and
so forth, with glazed boards, of various sizes, used
chiefly by printers, for pressing, which are manufactured in a peculiar manner by hand, the
boards being severally composed of various
sheets made in the ordinary way, but turned off
the mould one sheet upon another, until the
required substance be attained; a felt is then
placed upon the mass and another board formed.
By this means, the sheets, when pressed, adhere
more effectually to each other, and the boards
consequently become much more durable than
would be the case if they were produced by
pasting. Indeed, if any great amount of heat be
applied to pasteboards, they will split, and be
rendered utterly useless. The glazing in this
case is accomplished by friction.

To complete the category of coarse papers, I

ought to mention, as coming within the range of the Excise, Milled Boards, employed in bookbinding, of not less than one hundred and fifty descriptions, that is, as regards sizes and substances. Still, however, an incomplete idea is conveyed of the extraordinary number of sizes and descriptions into which paper is at present divided. For instance, I have said with reference to writing qualities, that there are *five* kinds, cream wove, yellow wove, blue wove, cream laid, and blue laid, and again, that of each of those kinds there are numerous sizes; but in addition there are, as a matter of course, various thicknesses and makes of each size and kind. In fact, no house in London, carrying on the wholesale stationery trade, is without a thousand different sorts; many keep stock of twice that number.

So much having of late been said with reference to a repeal of what are termed "Taxes on Knowledge," occasioning thereby many very erroneous opinions, it may be useful to offer some remarks upon Excise Regulations in connection with the duty on paper. And, in adverting to those regulations, we shall have an opportunity for observing the gradual increase which has taken place in the consumption, which in some measure tends to illustrate national advancement in the arts and sciences, and the general extension of literary pursuits. The Excise duty on paper was first imposed in the reign of Queen Anne. The statute, bearing date 1711, recites as a reason for the grant—which no doubt corresponds with that of *our* Chancellor of the Exchequer for its continuance—"the necessity of raising large supplies of money to carry on the present war, until your Majesty shall be enabled to establish a good and lasting peace." The duties at that time were charged on the ream, at rates varying according to the kind of paper, which was for this purpose divided into numerous denominations or classes, thus—"That there shall be raised, levyed, collected, and paid to and for the use of her Majesty, her heires and successors, for and upon all paper of what kind soever—— which shall at any time or times within, or during the terme of 32 years, to be reckoned from the foure and twentieth day of June, one thousand seven hundred and twelve, be made in Great Britaine, the severall and respective duties hereinafter menconed, that is to say, for and upon all paper usually called or knowne by the name of demy fine, which shall be soe made in Great Britaine, the sume of one shilling and six- pence for every reame, and after that rate for a greater or lesser quantity." And in like manner it goes on, fixing the amount per ream to be paid for second demy, fine and second crown, fine and second foolscap, fine and second pott, brown, large cap, small ordinary brown, whited brown, pasteboards, and lastly, " For and upon all other paper, white or browne, or of any other colour or kind whatsoever, which shall be made in Great Britaine as aforesaid, (not being particularly charged in this Act,) a duty after the rate of twelve pounds for every one hundred pounds of the true and reall value of the same, and after that rate for any greater or lesser quantities, which said duties for and upon the said severall sorts of paper and other the commodities last menčoned to be made in Great Britaine, shall be paid by the makers thereof respectively." But this method of drawing distinctions between different qualities and sizes of paper, being found to lead to frequent disputes with the Excise, and great inequality in the charge on the manufactured article at different mills, alterations were gradually made, till at length it was enacted in the 43rd year of the reign of George III., " that all paper and pasteboards should be considered first class, and subject to 3d. per lb. duty, unless made wholly out of old tarred rope and cordage, without extracting therefrom the pitch or tar, or any part thereof," and the Act further

says, " and without any mixture of other materials
therewith ;" and "that for every pound weight
avoirdupois of paper made in Great Britain, of
the second class or denomination, that is to say,
all brown paper made of old ropes or cordage
only, as aforesaid, a duty of 1½d. per lb. The
professed object of the last mentioned Act being
a simplification of the mode of charging the
duties, the numerous distinct classes into which
paper had been divided being here reduced to
two. But again, evasion of the law was soon
discovered to be practicable. Either by a partial
purification of the tarred rope, selecting also that
which was most whitened by use and exposure,
and then charging the paper so made (which was
nearly equal to first class in marketable value)
with the second class duty ; or as tarred rope
increased in price, and some sorts of first class
material very considerably declined, the great
temptation of an extensive evasion of the law
necessarily followed, by the use of first class
material in second class paper.

Whether the duty on paper as now imposed,
or the Excise regulations under which that duty
is collected, be the more objectionable, is perhaps
difficult to say. Of course, the paper-maker is
subjected to considerable annoyance, and the
publisher compelled to submit to an outlay which

he deems unjust, and would very happily dispense
with; but the public are not really affected by it
to the extent it is customary to suppose.   The
duty at present levied upon paper of all kinds is
fourteen guineas per ton, or a little more than
three halfpence per lb.   When, therefore, we hear
men pronouncing it "a most obnoxious tax," and
one "directly opposed to the advancement of
literature," I freely confess that, for my own part,
I hesitate very much to reiterate their sentiments.

Some, however, prefer an intermediate course,
and propose a *partial* abolition of the duty.   Mr.
Charles Dickens has favoured us with a suggestion to this effect: he says, "In England, where
coloured paper is so little used, the Chancellor of
the Exchequer might as well, as not, take off the
duty altogether from coloured paper.   It would
cost the revenue a mere trifle, while it would be a
vast boon to the public."   But what induces this
assertion ?   If coloured paper is so little used, the
trifling reduction could not be considered a *vast
boon*.   And one would like to know how or where
it would be possible to draw a line of distinction
between such papers as are coloured and those
which are not.   I happen to be in a position to
assert that there is no class of paper whatever,
which is not tinted more or less by different manufacturers.   To suggest then a partial repeal of the

duty upon such grounds, is, I apprehend, useless. If it had been confessed that the reduction would be a boon to the publisher, I should promptly have assented, simply because I am equally well aware that printing paper may be slightly tinted, with considerable advantage both as regards setting off the type, and the general appearance of a work; consequently if such really were to the public a boon, to the publisher it would be very considerably increased.

However, in order that we may not be supposed to lean to the present regulations, I shall refer to one or two clauses of the Act which I have no doubt will suffice to show, that while in itself it is very far from perfect in its operation, as protecting the interests of those concerned, it is equally unsatisfactory, and in some respects unjust.

I shall observe, that with regard to the Tax itself, I simply question whether it would be possible to impose one less injurious to the well-being of society, and against which, as of necessity, fewer persons could have cause to murmur, than the existing duty on paper. The sections of the Act to which I content myself with calling attention, are *three*, affecting the convenience and interest of the manufacturer, and *one* which offers a ready opportunity for an act of seeming dishonesty.

Every step of the manufacture of paper must be conducted under the surveillance of the Excise, and the provisions as to entries, folding, weighing, sorting, labelling, removing, and so on, are not only exceedingly numerous and vexatious, but enforced under heavy penalties. For instance, every paper maker is required by sections 20 & 21, to provide suitable scales and weights for the use of the Excise, and also to assist the officer in what we might conceive to be the execution of his peculiar duty, under the penalties, in the former case of £100., and in the latter, £50. for every refusal or neglect. To many manufacturers the cost of this extra labour alone becomes an important consideration.

Again, in the instance of procuring the Excise labels, which have to be pasted on each ream, section 9 requires that every one signed for by the workman on delivery, must be produced or accounted for, under a penalty of £10. each, which is equal to the duty upon no less than 1600 lbs. weight of paper; an idea necessarily inconsistent with that of its being packed in one parcel; and therefore, since for every time we divide such quantity, an additional label is required, a very forcible argument against so excessive a penalty may readily be deduced.

The labels employed are of three colours,—

red, blue, and green; denoting in which part of the kingdom the paper was made. Red being used for England; blue, for Scotland; and green for Ireland.

The 27th section of the Act, relating to the real and nominal weight of each ream or parcel, is that to which I have referred as being liable to deceptive or dishonest purposes. It runs thus —"And be it enacted—That if any ream, &c., be found to weigh under or over the weight marked, in the proportion of 5 per centum, if the weight marked on such ream exceed twenty pounds, or 10 per centum if such weight be twenty pounds or less, the same shall be forfeited.

Of course there is no necessity for a proviso lest the maker should give a preference to an increase of weight upon that marked, but since some cylinder dried papers are apt afterwards to increase in weight, the addition is requisite to prevent unjust seizure. However, in all probability, at the suggestion of the paper maker, when aiding the Excise, in consequence of a great quantity to be charged, it has become customary to average the weight of a draft, instead of putting each ream separately into the scale. Thus the practicability of rendering this clause highly objectionable will be at once apparent, and deserves to be pointed out for the purpose of warning against the temptation.

The quantity of paper manufactured in this country at the commencement of the eighteenth century, when the duty was first imposed, appears to have been far from sufficient to meet the necessities of the time.   Even in 1721, it is supposed that there were but about 300,000 reams of paper annually produced in Great Britain, which were equal merely to two-thirds of the consumption. But in 1784, the value of the paper manufactured in England alone is stated to have amounted to £800,000.; and that, by reason of the increase in price, as also of its use, in less than twenty years, it nearly doubled that amount.

I have extracted, from a Parliamentary report, various returns relating to the Excise duties levied upon paper, which, since an article of the kind is necessarily subjected to great alteration in value, according to the scarcity or abundance of raw materials, are, of course, better calculated to show a steady increase in the demand, than any mere references to statements of supposed value, from time to time.

In one return, specifying the rates of duty and amount of duty received upon each denomination of paper since 1770, it appears that the total amount of duty on paper manufactured in England for the year 1784, to which I have just alluded as being estimated in value at £800,000., was £46,867. 19s. 9¼d., the duty at that time being

divided into seven distinct classes or rates of collection; while twenty years after, when the mode
of assessing the duty was reduced to but three
classes, it had risen to £315,802. 4s. 8d.; in
1830, fifteen years after, to £619,824. 7s. 11d.; in
1835, for the United Kingdom, to £833,822. 12s.
4d., or, in weight, to 70,655,287lbs., which was,
again, within so short a period as fifteen years,
very nearly doubled. The quantity of paper
charged with Excise duty in the United Kingdom, being, in 1850, no less than 141,032,474lbs.,
and last year (1854) the enormous weight of
179,896,222lbs.

Those observations, which are partly technical,
because, without technicality, the view would be
incomplete,—may give some idea of the skill
required in the workman, and the expenditure
demanded of the capitalist, to produce so simple
a thing, as a sheet of paper. The most exact care,
the most ingenious invention, the nicest work of
hand, and the most complicated machinery, are
essential to that superiority which the British
manufacture of paper has at length established.

But the capabilities of paper are still more
extensive. There are probably few branches of
use, taste, or ornament, to which it may not be
applicable. We have it already moulded into
many forms of utility, and even of elegance,

I

under the well-known name of *papier mache*—
a material which may yet be formed into works
of art, painted and enamelled tables, antique
candelabra, models of busts, statuettes, classic
temples, and everything which can be shaped in
a mould.

An earlier and more important use of Paper is
in the decoration of dwellings. Formerly, the
apartments of persons of opulence were hung with
tapestry, generally brought from the Continental
loom. But its cost, its loss of colour by time;
and the rise of commercial and industrial
opulence, displaced this elaborate and heavy
decoration, and substituted " *paper hangings.*"
The first specimens of those exhibited nothing
but the rudeness of an art in its infancy, and
were almost wholly foreign; but the capability
of the invention was large, and it had the
advantage of converting the humble covering
of walls into copies of the pencil, on a new
and extended scale. The Continental specimens
of this manufacture already display representa-
tions of leading national events, memorable
battles, and even portraits of eminent men,
forming, for even the humbler ranks, a kind of
historic galleries.

The English manufacturer excels in the proportions of his paper, (English, 12 yards long,

by 21 inches wide; French, 9 yards, by 18 inches). But, the art is still difficult and costly; the blocks for a single pattern sometimes amounting to thousands. One of the principal French manufacturers is, at present, producing a design, requiring upwards of three thousand blocks, at a cost of £2000., the design alone costing £1200.

But, time and practice will lighten both the difficulty and the expense. The manufacture may yet spread through every mart in the world. In its more advanced stage, it may supply the place of FRESCO, or rather be a multiplied Fresco.

The Cartoons of Raphael, the noblest work of design, are upon paper; the finest Italian pictures might be copied upon paper; and the tardy and toilsome work of the Engraver might be exchanged for the rapid, cheap, and popular design, no longer limited to the palace or the cloister, but sent, in thousands of copies, round the globe. Nor let this be called Utopian; what can be Utopian, in the country of the Railroad, the Steam-ship, and the Electric Telegraph!

The art wants only public encouragement. Let the encouragement be given, and the talent will be found. Let Government offer a premium of even a thousand pounds for the best specimen. Let the Society of Arts make it one of the objects of their patronage; let it be once favoured, and it will soon advance to excellence.

Nor let any one scoff at the interest, which I venture to express in the ornament even of a cottage wall. Ornament is the crown of art. Taste is thought. Elegance is the refinement of civilization. The study of beauty, grandeur, and truth, in History and in Nature, is the most practical education of man! Who shall say, that the sight of some heroic action—some noble figure of history—some sublime exercise of talent, magnanimity, or patriotism, pictured on a cottage wall,—may not be like a flash through the darkness of the peasant heart; may not suddenly awake the latent energy of the unconscious poet, the patriot, and the hero; may not give to the world a Shakespeare, a Wallace, or a Wellington!

ADVERTISEMENT.

The Author desires to state for the information of the Subscribers, that
the delay which has arisen in the publication of this work has been
altogether unavoidable ; owing to the labour and difficulty of preparing such illustrations as were found to be necessary : many of
the Specimens inserted having been produced from moulds which
were manufactured expressly for the purpose.

LIST OF SUBSCRIBERS.

ADAMS, FRANCIS BRYANT, Esq., (Messrs. Charles Morgan and Co.)
AMOS, C. E., Esq., Consulting Engineer to the Royal Agricultural Society of England.
ANNANDALE, JAMES, Esq., Newcastle.
ANNANDALE, PETER, Esq., Newcastle.
APPOLD, J. G., Esq., F.R.S.

BALSTON, R. E. P., Esq., Maidstone.
BALSTON, WILLIAM, Esq., Maidstone.
BARING, THOMAS, Esq., M.P., F.R.G.S., &c., President of the London Institution.
BARLOW, THOMAS, Esq., Metropolitan Life Assurance Society.
BARRETT, RICHARD, Esq.
BARRY, SIR CHARLES, R.A., F.R.S., &c., &c.
BARRY, JAMES, Esq. (Messrs. Barry and Hayward.)
BATT, BENJAMIN, Esq.
BEAVIS, WILLIAM, Esq.
BEBBINGTON, H. A., Esq.
BLUNT, HENRY, Esq.
BRAYLEY, E. W., Esq., F.R.S., &c., &c.
BROOKMAN, WILLIAM, Esq., Romsey.
BROWN, RICHARD, Esq.
BROWNE, GEORGE, Esq.
BURR, T. W., Esq., F.R.A.S.

CARTER & BROMLEY, Messrs.
CHATER, GEORGE, Esq., (Messrs. Grosvenor, Chater and Co.)

COE, JOHN, Esq., Superintendent of the Stationery and Printing Department at the Bank of England.

COHEN, A., Esq.

COLES, HENRY, Esq., Wells, Somerset.

COLLINS, CHARLES, Esq., Hele, Devon.

CROMPTON, ROGER, Esq., Bolton, Lancashire.

COOKE, WAKEMAN E., Esq.

COOKES, JAMES, Esq.

COOPER, THOMAS, Esq. (Messrs. Williams, Coopers and Co.)

COWAN, CHARLES, Esq., M.P.

COWLEY, FREDERICK T., Esq.

CRANSTOUN, GEORGE C. TROTTER, Esq.

CROSBY, JAMES, Esq.

DAVIES, CHARLES, Esq.

DIGGENS, J. G , Esq., H. M. Stationery Office.

DRAPER, S., Esq.

DREW, WILLIAM, Esq., Bradninch, Devon.

DUNSTER, THOMAS, Esq.

EDITOR OF NOTES AND QUERIES.

EHRENSPERGER, C., & Co., Messrs.

EVANS AND ADLARD, Messrs., Birmingham.

EVANS, SAMUEL, & Co., Messrs., Derby.

FICKLING, W., Esq.

FOURDRINIER AND HUNT, Messrs.

GALE, A., Esq.

GALLON, THOMAS, & Co., Messrs., Gateshead.

GOOCH, EDWARD F., Esq.

GOWER, JOHN, Esq.

GRACE, WILLIAM, Esq., Scotswood.

GREENAWAY, EDWARD, Esq.

GREER, ALFRED, Esq., Cork.

HALE, FORD, Esq.

HALLOWS, W. A., Esq.

HAMMOND, CHARLES, Esq.

HARDY, T. DUFFUS, Esq., Record Office, Tower.
HARDY, JOHN SMART, Esq.
HARRIS, CHARLES, Esq., Countess Weir, Exeter.
HAWTIN, WILLIAM, Esq.
HAYLES, JAMES N., Esq.
HERRING, GEORGE, Esq.
HODGKINSON, WILLIAM SAMPSON, Esq.
HOLLINGWORTH, THOMAS, Esq., Maidstone.
HUSSEY, THOMAS E., Esq., Dudley.
HUTTON, THOMAS O., Esq. (Messrs. Millington & Hutton)

JEAFFRESON, HENRY, Esq., M.D.
JOHNSON, RICHARD, Esq.

KELLY, Rev. A. P., M.A.
KIDD, DAVID, Esq. (Messrs. Dobbs, Kidd and Co.)

LAWSON, F. L., Esq.
LE BLOND, ROBERT, Esq.
LUNNON, THOMAS, Esq., Wooburn.

MCMURRAY, WILLIAM, Esq., Hon. Sec. to the " Fourdrinier Fund."
MAGNAY, SIR WILLIAM, Baronet.
MARTYN, RICHARD, Esq., Broadclist, Devon.
MATTHEWS, CHARLES, Esq., Bradninch, Devon.
MILLINGTON, CHARLES, Esq.
MILLS, A. D., Esq.
MORGAN, CHARLES, Esq.
MORGAN, GEORGE, Esq.
MUNN, R. J., Esq., Thetford.
MURRELL, H. E., Esq.
MUSCHAMP, WILLIAM, Esq., Gateshead.

NEILL, JOHN, Esq., Leeds.
NICHOLL, JOHN, Esq., F.S.A.
NISSEN AND PARKER, Messrs.
NORRIS, JOHN THOMAS, Esq.

PAMPLIN, JAMES, Esq., Winchester.

PATTISON, T. S., Esq.
PEEBLES, ALEXANDER M. Esq.
PHELPS, J. B., Esq.
PIRIE, ALEXANDER, AND SONS, Messrs.
POLLARD, GEORGE, Esq.
POLLOCK, JOHN, Esq.
POPE, HENRY, Esq.
POULTER, THOMAS, Esq.
PRINCE, GEORGE, Esq.

RALPH, F. W. Esq.
RICHARD, JOHN EDMUND, Esq.
ROCK, WILLIAM FREDERICK, Esq.
ROCK, BROTHERS AND PAYNE, Messrs.
ROE, THOMAS, Esq. (Messrs. Gibbons and Roe.)
ROSSELLI, E. Esq.
RUSSELL, REV. SAMUEL HENRY, B D.

SAKER, WILLIAM E., Esq. Reading.
SANDELL, RICHARD B., Esq.
SAUNDERS, J. & E., Messrs.
SAUNDERS, T. H., Esq., Dartford.
SHAW, EDMUND, Esq.
SLADE, WILLIAM, Esq.
SMEE, ALFRED, Esq., F.R.S., F.C.S.
SMITH, JAMES, Esq.
SMITH, JOHN, Esq., Bingley.
SMITH, J. W., Esq., Bingley.
SMITH, JOHN, Esq., Langley.
SMITH, WILLIAM, Esq.
SMITH, WILLIAM LEPARD, AND CO., Messrs.
SOMMERVILLE, WILLIAM, Esq., Bitton.
SPALDING AND HODGE, Messrs.
STERRY, HENRY, Esq.

TANNER, R. T., Esq.
TARBOX, EDWARD, Esq.
TAYLOR, WILLIAM, Esq.
TEMPLETON, ALLAN, Esq.

TITE, WILLIAM, Esq., M.P., F.R.S., &c., &c.

TOOVEY, A. D., Esq.

TOWGOOD, ALFRED, Esq., Reading.

TOWGOOD, EDWARD, Esq., Sawston.

TOWGOOD, FREDERICK, Esq , St. Neots.

TOWN, JOSEPH, Esq., Leeds.

TULLIS AND CO., Messrs. R., Markinch, N.B.

TYLER, WILLIAM, Esq. (Messrs. Venables, Wilson and Tyler.)

VARTY, EDWARD, Esq.

VENABLES, GEORGE, Esq.

VINCENT, J. Esq.

WALL, JAMES, Esq.

WARREN, B. J., Esq., Deal.

WARREN, G. R., Esq., Bramshott.

WATSON, WILLIAM, Esq.

WEAKLIN, FREDERICK, Esq.

WEST, FREDERICK, Esq.

WHATMAN, JAMES, Esq., M.P., F.R.S., &c., &c., Maidstone

WHITE, EDWARD, Esq.

WHITAKER, THOMAS, Esq.

WILLIAMS, SAMUEL T., Esq.

WILLIAMS, ROBERT, Esq.

WILMOT, GEORGE, Esq., Shoreham.

WILSON, SAMUEL, Esq., Alderman, Lieutenant-Colonel of the Royal London Militia.

WINSTONE, BENJAMIN, Esq.

WIRE, DAVID WILLIAMS, Esq., Alderman of the Ward of Walbrook.

WOOD, DREW, Esq.

WOODWARD, CHARLES, Esq., F.R.S., President of the Islington Literary and Scientific Society.

YOUNG, JOHN T., Esq.

For EU product safety concerns, contact us at Calle de José Abascal, 56–1°,
28003 Madrid, Spain or eugpsr@cambridge.org.